MW00528221

JESUS
IN
THE
WILD

JESUS
IN
THE
WILD

Lessons

on Calling for

Life in the World

DAN WILT

Scripture quotations are taken from the Holy Bible, New International Version®,
NIV® Copyright © 1973, 1978, 1984, 2011 by Biblica, Inc.™ Used by permission
of Zondervan. All rights reserved worldwide. www.zondervan.com. The "NIV"
and "New International Version" are trademarks registered in the United States
Patent and Trademark Office by Biblica, Inc.™ All rights reserved worldwide.

Scripture quotations marked NCB are taken from the SAINT JOSEPH
NEW CATHOLIC BIBLE® Copyright © 2019 by Catholic Book
Publishing Corp. Used with permission. All rights reserved.

Printed in the United States of America

Cover design by Strange Last Name
Page design by PerfecType, Nashville, Tennessee

Wilt, Dan.
  Jesus in the wild : lessons on calling for life in the world /
Dan Wilt. – Franklin, Tennessee : Seedbed Publishing, ©2023.

    pages ; cm. + 1 video disc

    ISBN: 9781628249842 (paperback)
    ISBN: 9781628249927 (DVD)
    ISBN: 9781628249859 (mobi)
    ISBN: 9781628249866 (epub)
    ISBN: 9781628249873 (pdf)
    OCLC: 1350299365

    1. Jesus Christ--Temptation. 2. Bible. Luke, IV, 1-14--Criticism,
interpretation, etc. 3. Spiritual warfare. 4. Temptation--Religious
aspects--Christianity. 5. Vocation--Christianity. I. Title.

BT355.W54 2023   232.9/5   2022949643

SEEDBED PUBLISHING
Franklin, Tennessee
seedbed.com

CONTENTS

AN INVITATION TO AWAKENING

This resource comes with an invitation.

The invitation is as simple as it is comprehensive. It is not an invitation to commit your life to this or that cause or to join an organization or to purchase another book. The invitation is this: to wake up to the life you always hoped was possible and the reason you were put on planet Earth.

It begins with following Jesus Christ. In case you are unaware, Jesus was born in the first century BCE into a poor family from Nazareth, a small village located in what is modern-day Israel. While his birth was associated with extraordinary phenomena, we know little about his childhood. At approximately thirty years of age, Jesus began a public mission of preaching, teaching, and healing throughout the region known as Galilee. His mission was characterized by miraculous signs and wonders; extravagant care of the poor and marginalized; and multiple unconventional claims about his own identity and purpose. In short, he claimed to be the incarnate Son of God with the mission and power to save people from sin, deliver them from death, and bring them into the now and eternal kingdom of God—on earth as it is in heaven.

In the spring of his thirty-third year, during the Jewish Passover celebration, Jesus was arrested by the religious authorities, put on trial in the middle of the night, and at their urging, sentenced to death by a Roman governor. On the day known to history as Good Friday, Jesus was crucified on a Roman cross. He was buried in a borrowed tomb. On the following Sunday, according to multiple eyewitness accounts, he was physically raised from the dead. He appeared to hundreds of people, taught his disciples, and prepared for what was to come.

Forty days after the resurrection, Jesus ascended bodily into the heavens where, according to the Bible, he sits at the right hand of God, as the Lord of heaven and earth. Ten days after his ascension, in a gathering of 120 people on the day of Pentecost, a Jewish day of celebration, something truly extraordinary happened. A loud and powerful wind swept over the people gathered. Pillars of what appeared to be fire descended upon the followers of Jesus. The Holy Spirit, the presence and power of God, filled the people, and the church was born. After this, the followers of Jesus went forth and began to do the very things Jesus did—preaching, teaching, and healing—planting churches and making disciples all over the world. Today, more than two thousand years later, the movement has reached us. This is the Great Awakening and it has never stopped.

Yes, two thousand years hence and more than two billion followers of Jesus later, this awakening movement of Jesus Christ and his church stands stronger than ever. Billions of ordinary people the world over have discovered in Jesus Christ an awakened life they never imagined possible. They have overcome challenges, defeated addictions, endured untenable hardships and suffering with unexplainable joy, and stared death in the face with the joyful confidence of eternal life. They have healed the sick, gathered the outcasts, embraced the oppressed, loved the poor, contended for justice, labored for peace, cared for the dying, and yes, even raised the dead.

We all face many challenges and problems. They are deeply personal, yet when joined together, they create enormous and complex chaos in the world, from our hearts to our homes to our churches and our cities. All of this chaos traces to two originating problems: sin and death. Sin, far beyond mere moral failure, describes the fundamental broken condition of every human being. Sin separates us from God and others, distorts and destroys our deepest identity as the image-bearers of God, and poses a fatal problem from which we cannot save ourselves. It results in an ever-diminishing quality of life and ultimately ends in eternal death. Because Jesus lived a life of sinless perfection, he is able to save us from sin and restore us to a right relationship with God, others, and ourselves. He did this through his sacrificial death on the cross on our behalf. Because Jesus rose from the dead, he is able to deliver us from death and bring us into a quality of life both eternal and unending.

This is the gospel of Jesus Christ: pardon from the penalty of sin, freedom from the power of sin, deliverance from the grip of death, and awakening to the supernatural empowerment of the Holy Spirit to live powerfully for the good of others and the glory of God. Jesus asks only that we acknowledge our broken selves as failed sinners, trust him as our Savior, and follow him as our Lord. Following Jesus does not mean an easy life; however, it does lead to a life of power and purpose, joy in the face of suffering, and profound, even world-changing, love for God and people.

All of this is admittedly a lot to take in. Remember, this is an invitation. Will you follow Jesus? Don't let the failings of his followers deter you. Come and see for yourself.

Here's a prayer to get you started:

> Our Father in heaven, it's me (say your name), I want to know you. I want to live an awakened life. I confess I am a sinner. I have failed myself, others, and you in many ways. I know you made me for a purpose, and I want to fulfill that purpose with my one life. I want to follow Jesus

Christ. Jesus, thank you for the gift of your life and death and resurrection and ascension on my behalf. I want to walk in relationship with you as Savior and Lord. Would you lead me into the fullness and newness of life I was made for? I am ready to follow you. Come, Holy Spirit, and fill me with the love, power, and purposes of God. I pray these things by faith in the name of Jesus, amen.

It would be our privilege to help you get started and grow deeper in this awakened life of following Jesus. For some next steps and encouragements, visit seedbed.com/Awaken.

LESSONS ON CALLING FOR LIFE IN THE WORLD

When the Father calls you by name, there is always a threefold challenge that follows—a challenge to your identity, a challenge to your belovedness, and a challenge to your purpose.

That challenge comes from somewhere, from a spiritual foe who is the embodiment of evil, an enemy whose singular goal is to get you lost in the wilderness—lost about who you are (your identity), *whose* you are (your belovedness), and what you are for (your purpose).

I began to follow Christ during my high school years, spurred on by the encouragement and prayers of family members, a few faithful teachers, and some precious and discerning Christian friends.

I was loved to life in those early years of walking with Jesus. I vibrantly felt my faith, fresh and growing, at work in my bones. The Spirit was conforming me to Jesus, even while I slept. I experienced sonship, an abiding and quieting awareness of my identity as a child of God, and my purpose that flowed from that relationship of love. In those days, I experienced the heart-conquering and winsome affection of God, and a strange lifting of heavy weights that had been oppressing my spirit.

I gave everything I had to follow Jesus; it seemed the only fitting response to such great love. There have been many delightful days and dark nights since then. One would think, having experienced such astounding acceptance, affirmation, and blessing—in such a profound way, for so many decades—that I would never look back.

But in the wilderness seasons of life, when we feel lost and abandoned, we sometimes look back.

AFTER THE BLESSING COMES THE TEMPTATION

I looked back, many times over the decades of my life. I looked back when the going got tough, when the emotions ran dry, or when a whisper—a beautiful but evil whisper—asked me "if" I was *actually* precious to God.

It goes something like this: *If you are precious to God, then why is this happening to you?*

When one is in the midst of a protracted season of suffering, despair over our situation, or affliction with a chronic illness, that "if" seems to ring louder than all the worship songs one has ever sung.

If.

The battle to get us to look back begins the day we first embrace our identity, our belovedness, our purpose, our vocation—spoken to us intimately by the Father. As soon as that happens, as soon as love floods our soul and we say yes to the name God gives us, there is a satanic presence lurking in the background, waiting for an "opportune time" (Luke 4:13) to woo us away.

When and what are those opportune times? Moments of vulnerability, insecurity, pain, success, failure, insufficiency, pride, unbelief, confusion, despair, lust, greed, or revenge.

And, if we let our enemy, our adversary, the one the Bible calls "the satan"—meaning "the adversary"—(I will refer to our enemy that biblical way throughout this book) draw us away from our true name before God, we will go down a slow track of confusion, disorientation, and even self-hatred and self-destruction.

The ancient spoke of the two ways, the path to life and the path to death (Deut. 30:19; Ps. 16:11). For every person, that path to death begins the day we believe even a single word the devil speaks. It begins the day we listen to the enemy's voice, without a heaven-powered refusal addressing the voice immediately and head-on. Listening to the evil one's voice, both metaphorically and literally, is suicide. It all begins with one temptation left unanswered.

JESUS IN THE WILD

Since the time of my conversion, more than forty years ago now, I have been fascinated by the story of Jesus in the wilderness in Luke 4:1–14.

I have always felt there was more to that story than met the eye. I've heard myriad messages on those verses, and I've preached on that passage many times throughout the decades. I've spent hours reflecting on not only the passage, but also on what it means for Jesus to have been the one to pass on this story to his disciples (and all who would follow them). After all, no one else was with Jesus in the desert to record it; Jesus must have shared this profound experience with his followers, most probably to equip them for their own challenges ahead.

All that time, I now humbly confess, I have been reading the story from a limited perspective—along with many in the body of Christ, I'm sure. I won't say that my reading of the wilderness narrative had been *completely* wrong, but I will say that I usually missed the wider, all-important context of Luke 3 and 4 in which the story takes place.

The story of Jesus in the wilderness—or Jesus in the "wild," as I like to call the untamed places where life tumbles into life along our journey—is all about vocation (from the Latin word *vocare*, which means "to call"). Vocation is what we speak of as a "calling." How to receive our calling, embrace our calling, and fulfill our calling is the vital truth that sits at the center of the journey ahead of us.

What happened between when Jesus was blessed and called into his vocation at his baptism and when Jesus launched into the fullness of his ministry in Luke 4:14–21 (see Isa. 61:1–2)? What happened between the naming and the doing, the calling and the ministry?

What happened was the wild. And what happens in the wild is what determines the *telos* (end goal) of your life and mine.

For that reason, I've wanted to revisit the treasures in this story many times over the years. Now is the opportunity, and I am grateful you can join me on the journey of discovery before us.

A SEASON OF SCRIPTURE MEDITATION

We're about to share a long revisitation, a lengthy and moving meditation, on Luke 4:1–14. In the spirit of the ancient monastic practice of *lectio divina*, a practice marked by the continued repetition of a passage so one begins to not only enter the truth of the passage, but also to allow the Spirit to have the passage enter us, we will proceed.

In other words, I'd like to invite you to meditate on this *one* story in the Gospels for an *entire season*. To enter this passage, to enter it deeply and with a view to receive understanding and revelation as to its meaning for the church and for each one of us, will be transforming. I believe this because the "Word of God is living and active" (Heb. 4:12) and will be used by the Spirit to trigger seismic soul shifts in us—shifts we may not be aware are happening along the way.

It bears noting that the Hebrew word for meditation (as in "*meditates* on his law day and night" in Psalm 1:2) is the word *hagah*. This rich word hosts within it the idea that it is by mulling over, repeating continually, chewing on (like a dog with a bone), and lingering in passages from the Word of God, the Scriptures give up their layered and thick truth to us as we savor their words and meaning.

That is what we will do together over the course of these pages with the story of Jesus in the wilderness.

We will plumb the depths of this passage by lingering in one word, or one phrase, for the space of a single entry. Then, as we explore other words and phrases in these fourteen powerful verses, they will compound into a multilayered, thick truth over time. We will return again and again to the ideas explored in the previous days as we add to our opening passage daily.

Mulling, repeating, chewing, lingering—these are fitting verbs for how we must handle the Word of Truth (2 Tim. 2:15) and its Spirit-revealed implications for walking on the path of life (Ps. 16:11).

VOCATION: BEING, BECOMING, AND DOING

Our meditation will center on the powerful biblical idea of vocation—what it means to be called by God to a purpose—and then to stay with that purpose through the hard days and deep nights we call a lifetime.

Jesus had to do this. So do we.

I will use the terms *vocation* and *calling* interchangeably throughout the book, but the term vocation will take the lead.

From my perspective, our vocation is a powerful way of expressing the idea of calling in our lives. However, when Christ-followers speak of calling with other Christ-followers, we often talk about the idea as a vague sense of purpose to do something, accomplish something, or get something done in the world.

Putting *doing* before *being* or, more accurately, making *doing* our foundation and *being* an optional add-on, we can create a monster. An affirmation-addiction monster. An applause-seeking monster. A misuse-of-power monster. A self-preservation monster. Monsters beget monsters, and our work, with Jesus as our leader, is to undo the hellish effects of the leading monster at work in the world (1 John 3:8).

Our vocation, a divine treasure given to each one of us from birth and originating in creation itself, is an invitation to be someone who then does something in the world.

Your vocation is to *be* someone who *does* something in the world.

Let that sink in.

If I don't know who I am, who I am to become—then I will endlessly wander, trying to figure out what I am to do in the world.

Being leads to *becoming* leads to *doing*—a progression which leads to further awareness of who we are, who we are becoming, and what we are to do.

Jesus knew who he was (*being*), who he was being formed to be for the future of humankind (*becoming*), and what he was to accomplish in the world his Father loves (*doing*).

THE WILD IS A PLACE OF TESTING

And that leads us to the story of Jesus in the wild and what happened there.

The wilderness, according to the Bible, is the *eremos*—it speaks of a place of isolation, separation, and encounter. We'll explore this word later.

And just what was that experience that Jesus had?

Jesus was tested, and that test came by way of three temptations from the devil. If you struggle with the idea that the Father allows us to be tested, then read through the Old Testament and consider how many tests of faith, devotion, courage, and obedience were presented for those who loved God and were "called according to his purpose" (Rom. 8:28).

God allows us to be tested for our good. The enemy, however, tempts us for our destruction. The two experiences can look similar, but the purposes and outcomes of each are very, very different. God's testing is intended to build us up. The enemy's tempting is intended to tear us down.

In between our profound encounters with the God who is love (Jesus will encounter his Father in this way in his baptism in Luke 3) and some of the most profound vocational ministry activity of our lives (Jesus will leave the wilderness to minister in the "power of the [Holy] Spirit" in Luke 4:14), there will be a test.

Biblical scholar Tim Mackie (of Bible Project) illuminates what a test is for us. The Greek word is *periazo*—a test that reveals the truth of something[1]—and that test will somehow involve both God's divine purpose and the enemy's destructive challenge. Like tests in school, a test reveals what is, what we know, what is true and behind the veil of impressions. Tests reveal truth about our character, and are meant for our good. Temptations (another way the word is translated) have the goal of leading us to do evil.

Abraham was tested. Israel was tested. And Jesus was tested by the Pharisees to reveal the truth about who he was. Mackie suggests that we must welcome the idea that God tests people in ways that reveal what is happening inside us. I have come to agree.

How we handle those tests, and who we see those tests coming from, means everything; our heart is being proved true and our faith revealed as genuine (1 Peter 1:7) in such times of difficulty.

When our soul has been tested and we pass, we internally become convinced that something has actually become *real* within. In those moments, God has used the challenge to show us our own hearts and to convince us that we are indeed living truly according to what we believe. With such a self-convincing revelation pounding at our core, we can become an unstoppable force of life and love in the world.

But when our faith remains in the land of questions, the lands of ifs and maybes, and we wonder if we have what it takes to see this

---

1. Tim Mackie, "Testing Jesus in the Wilderness," Bible Project, YouTube.com, August 19, 2017, https://youtu.be/nur0SFmH--0.

whole, strange faith thing through until the end, then we are impotent to press through the hell before us to see the heaven rising behind it.

I would encourage you to have a journal open and ready as you read each entry, to note words or phrases that are meaningful to you, as well as to answer the questions that are at the conclusion of each reading. It is widely known in Christian history that through journaling and writing, the Holy Spirit helps us to both document and remember words we are given to carry forward into our future.

As we consider this passage, we will be meditating on the story in the historic and prayerful spirit of contemplation, being with God in conversation as we read.[2] Eugene Peterson speaks of contemplation this way: "Contemplation in the schema of *lectio divina* means living the read/meditated/prayed text in the everyday, ordinary world. It means getting the text into our muscles and bones, our oxygen-breathing lungs and blood-pumping heart."[3]

I agree with Peterson; we must eat this story, and it must become part of us.

Your journal will provide a lasting record that you invested your own heart into this season at the feet of Jesus, and that you addressed the demonic and satanic voices that were challenging

---

2. A. J. Sherrill, *Being with God: The Absurdity, Necessity, and Neurology of Contemplative Prayer* (Grand Rapids, MI: Brazos Press, 2021), 18.
3. Eugene Peterson, *Eat This Book: A Conversation in the Art of Spiritual Reading* (Grand Rapids, MI: William B. Eerdmans, 2009), 109.

you in your own vocation before God. Your journal will be a lasting record that you came out on the other side of this reading stronger in heart for the next season of life and ministry in the Holy Spirit.

Yours for the awakening,
Dan Wilt

JESUS IN THE WILD

LUKE 4:1–14

Jesus, full of the Holy Spirit, left the Jordan and was led by the Spirit into the wilderness, where for forty days he was tempted by the devil. He ate nothing during those days, and at the end of them he was hungry.

The devil said to him, "If you are the Son of God,
tell this stone to become bread."

Jesus answered, "It is written: 'Man shall not live on bread alone.'"

The devil led him up to a high place and showed him in an instant all the kingdoms of the world. And he said to him, "I will give you all their authority and splendor; it has been given to me, and I can give it to anyone I want to. If you worship me, it will all be yours."

Jesus answered, "It is written: 'Worship the Lord
your God and serve him only.'"

The devil led him to Jerusalem and had him stand on the highest point of the temple. "If you are the Son of God," he said, "throw yourself down from here. For it is written:

"'He will command his angels concerning you
to guard you carefully;
they will lift you up in their hands,
so that you will not strike your foot against a stone.'"

Jesus answered, "It is said: 'Do not put the Lord your God to the test.'"

When the devil had finished all this tempting,
he left him until an opportune time.

Jesus returned to Galilee in the power of the Spirit, and news
about him spread through the whole countryside.

Life is more wild than tame, more surprising than predictable—and God works within this mystery.

Consider, with me, the following word groups. Group 1: *tame, predictable, comfortable, safe, sustainable, content, peaceful, reliable, sure, rest.* Group 2: *wild, unpredictable, uncomfortable, dangerous, unsustainable, adventurous, alert, surprising, unsure, restless.*

Which group of words is more immediately attractive to you?

If you are like me, I would *like* to say that Group 2 is more appealing; it feels more noble and more adventurous to do so. But, to be honest, I need to say that Group 1 really has my heart. Having my heart, it also has my bank account, my relational patterns, and the lion's share of my daily choices.

Why choose the wild and unpredictable when the tame and comfortable is right there beside it?

Are you heavily invested in creating a Group 1 life—a life that is tame, predictable, peaceful, sustainable, and sure? Do your habits reflect it? Does your job reflect it? Do your relationships and the way you handle them reflect it?

Now, here comes the big question: Does the way you follow Jesus reflect it?

Even those who have mastered their mechanisms for controlling their lives find the experience from birth to death *wild*—untamed, unruly, unpredictable, and downright inhospitable at moments. Life in motion overtakes our best-laid plans, our best-planned futures, and can lead those plans into chaos without frequent intervention and constant maintenance.

If you are like some of my acquaintances over the years, you may choose a highly controlled life with little risk and tightly managed relationships. But even for them—*surprises*. Pandemics. Social unrest. Political upheaval. Personal crises. Prisons of the heart, mind, and body—so many challenges break through and touch the most heavily fortified soul.

But along the way of growing up in Christ—and by that I mean the *long* growing up that takes decades and sculpts the spirit—we make a discovery.

Life is, by nature, unpredictable. It is what we will call "wild." It is when life is unpredictable that we most quickly discover who God is and who we are in him.

Thomas Merton, when speaking of the early desert fathers—those who chose a wild and unpredictable life when the empire became Christianized—wrote: "What the fathers sought most of all was their true self, in Christ. And in order to do this, they had to reject completely the false, formal self, fabricated under social compulsion 'in the world.'"[4]

The Holy Spirit does an incredible work in us when things feel most precarious, unsafe, and unpredictable. The Spirit reveals to us, and affirms, our calling. No, we don't all have to run away from the empire of the world in order to find our calling, but we do need to recognize that drifting into acceptance of the status quo can slowly, but surely, kill us.

Another word for *calling*—or invitation from God to participate with him uniquely as we truly are in the world—is *vocation*.

---

4. Thomas Merton, *The Wisdom of the Desert* (Trappist, KY: The Abbey of Gethsemani, Inc., 1960), 5–6.

Vocation, from the Latin word *vocare*, means "to call." In the wild, in the unpredictable and ever-changing, we are listening hard for the voice of God. And when we are listening hard, often because it is hard, we hear the voice of God. And that makes all the difference.

The wild is a place of naked encounter with God and ourselves. It is the place we never want to go—but we choose to go there because the Spirit has led us there and we are not content to remain as we are.

In Luke 4:1–14, Jesus enters that place of the wild, the unpredictable, the isolated, for a purpose—a vocational purpose. It is a dangerous place for him to be—but as we will see, it is the right place. And if it was the right place for him, for a time and for an eternal purpose, the wild is the right place for us for times and purposes in our lives that are yet to be discovered.

God can be encountered anywhere. The wild, in its unruliness, in its lack of clear promise, with its sense of missed or averted destiny, is a unique place of encounter and formation for the follower of Christ.

With Jesus, let's enter the wilderness, led by the Spirit.

THE PRAYER

Lord of the Wild, we sense the possibility that is in store for us if we take this season to walk with you into the revelation that awaits us in the story of your testing in the wilderness. Open our hearts to hear your Spirit's voice, to be led by the Spirit into an encounter with you that ends in your love and power being more fully manifest in our lives and in a new clarity of our vocation in you. In Jesus's name, amen.

DAN WILT

- Have you experienced the wild in recent weeks? If so, how has the unpredictability, the lack of control you've felt, revealed where your faith is really at?

JESUS

LUKE 4:1

Jesus, full of the Holy Spirit, left the Jordan and was
led by the Spirit into the wilderness . . .

CONSIDER THIS

Jesus is the name his Father in heaven gave him; and to the
Hebrews, a name means everything.

What is known as the wilderness of Israel—the wild, unruly, and
untamed barren land of this part of the world—is devoid of life,
food, and water.

The wild was a dangerous place to be. Into the wilderness of
testing, armed with only the name and vocation his Father had
affirmed at his baptism, Jesus went.

Jesus. Humans need salvation. Look at what we do to ourselves,
to one another. These hearts and their tears need resolve, drying,
healing. We live. We love. We desire. We dream. We also kill. We
hate. We lust. We create nightmares from our desire to shape the
world according to our own designs. As Augustine explained it,

our desires are disordered,[5] and we fail ourselves and others when we try to live without a Savior at work within us.

Into this world, yours and mine, a Savior comes—a representative human. He models, in heart, in mind, in body, in purpose, what it means to live the truly good life. In his shining model, we see virtues that stand in stark contrast to the vices given sacred status by the world.

Jesus, the "Lord saves," is the Savior given to us. He will face it all, all the horrors of the heart that we face as children of Adam and Eve, and will do it without breaking covenant with the Creator (Heb. 4:15). He will do, in his test in the wilderness, what Israel could not on its own.

Flesh and blood, Jesus moved in the world, grew up in a family, and became a young man. Then, in his thirties, he makes his move. Showing up at the baptismal waters of John, Jesus gets his business card from the Father.

"When all the people were being baptized, Jesus was baptized too. And as he was praying, heaven was opened and the Holy Spirit descended on him in bodily form like a dove. And a voice came from heaven: 'You are my Son, whom I love; with you I am well pleased'" (Luke 3:21–22).

"You are my Son"—Jesus's core identity and vocation is clear: to live as a Son in perfect covenant communion with his Father. Jesus knows who he is.

"Whom I love"—Jesus receives, at the beginning of his ministry, a word of affection and belovedness that will feed him the rest of his life. Jesus knows whose he is.

---

5. Augustine, *Confessions* 4. 10.15.

"With you I am well pleased"—Jesus receives an affirmation of his value before he has even done one miracle. Jesus knows why he is and what he must do that flows from it—he will not draw his sense of purpose from anything other than the Father's love.

His vocation, his calling, his core identity, his essential nature, is blessed and secured by the Father.

After his time in the desert wild in Luke 4:18–20, he will stand to read the scroll of Isaiah and declare that the scripture has been fulfilled in their hearing. He will inaugurate the kingdom coming with this blessing and unveil it in his ministry.

But between Jesus's baptism and kingdom proclamation from Isaiah lies the wild.

Jesus's experience in the wild in Luke 4 is different from suffering or even just temptation. I was taught to conflate the two ideas of the wilderness and suffering, and though testing from all sides happens in all kinds of trials, the wild Jesus enters is a Spirit-led challenge on a field of battle into which he has been guided by the breath of God.

He has just had his name blessed, his belovedness settled, his intrinsic value affirmed in baptism (3:21–22). Now, that vocation, that belovedness, that sense of value—all established on covenant love with the Father—is about to be tested.

Tested? Does God test his people in the Bible? Did God test Abraham, Moses, his people Israel? Absolutely. The wild, the place of testing, can even be one we *choose*. Jesus is isolated and empty (fasting) by choice to face down the sinister voice that is about to tell him that everything God has said is untrue, and that there is a better way. Do you know that voice? I know that voice.

Jesus goes into the wild to face the enemy without the crowd or even his mother, Mary, to psych him up. It is him, full of the Holy Spirit, facing down the needling questions the enemy has prepared.

He will come out of this wilderness; we now know with the benefit of having the whole story laid before us. But for Jesus, there was no "next part of Luke" to read. He was going into a dangerous place where he would have to entertain the most basic, unsettling, and selfhood-challenging questions of his entire life. To be tested means we could fail.

Jesus will not fail.

And if he can face those questions down now as he goes into the wild, and answer them solidly for his own heart, he can walk the hard road ahead of him.

THE PRAYER

Lord of the Wild, we don't choose to go places where danger might meet us. But in your story, we see the Spirit leading you into a place of risk and challenge. Give us the grace to be led by you into places that may challenge us, but that will also prove that faith is alive in our hearts. In Jesus's name, amen.

THE QUESTIONS

- Is there a wilderness you sense the Holy Spirit has led you into recently that is calling into question your faith and confidence in who God has called you to be? How are you doing so far?

3

FULL

LUKE 4:1

Jesus, *full* of the Holy Spirit, left the Jordan and was
led by the Spirit into the wilderness . . .

CONSIDER THIS

We can look empty and remain hungry, while at the same time being as full as we've ever been.

Jesus goes into the wilderness, not with his belly full of food, but with his heart full of the Holy Spirit. He is prepared to go without food, because he is drawing from a source that satisfies more than his bodily cravings. Fasting can have that effect on us.

Fullness. You know that feeling you have when you have just had a good meal and you are completely satisfied with no need to further satiate your palate or your hunger? That is one form of fullness. Do you know that other feeling when you have just been with those you love and you exchanged the gifts of care, warmth, and support? That is another form of fullness.

Jesus is full of something when he leaves the Jordan of his baptism and heads toward the wilderness led by the Spirit. Food may set his endorphins in motion, but Jesus is resisting the satisfaction of food in order to make his spirit attentive to a different kind of good. He wants to be full of something else.

I believe he is full of love—the Father's satisfying, satiating, spiritual-hunger-quenching *love*. That is what Jesus's baptism was all about. That is why Jesus spends his entire ministry unmoved by the fickle opinions of the crowd. He has learned to feed from God's presence and love rather than from affirmation and attention. That "learned indifference," as Ignatius of Loyola called it, enabled him to be indifferent to anything other than the Father's will.

In John 4:32 Jesus says to his inquisitive disciples, "I have food to eat that you know nothing about." When they press him to understand where he got a meal, Jesus explains in verse 34: "My food . . . is to do the will of him who sent me and to finish his work."

The Holy Spirit confers the Father's love to the heart. We can be full, before the crowd puts us on a stage. There is no other way to be full entering an empty world. If you haven't learned to find your fullness in God's presence, you will find an unsatisfying fullness when the world offers you another option. Many look for love in the crowd, in social media likes, in relationships, and in other fountains.

But the psalmist said in Psalm 87:7, "All my fountains are in you."

Jesus had found the fountain of life—the true fountain that fills the waiting spirit.

People in this world settle for all kinds of loves—romantic love, sexual love, friendship love, celebrity love, pet love, love of country, love of spouse, even family love—to satisfy their unspoken desire for divine love. Some of these may have their place, but all are disordered desires until we understand their context within the great love of God.

The enemy can challenge your calling and mine, when our loves are out of order, with ease. When we find our satisfaction, our fullness, in anything other than the love of God, we are an easy target in the wild. We question God's love, we follow false idols, and we do injustice out of self-protection—all because our hearts have found fullness, equivalent to a spiritual emptiness, in a love lesser than the love of God for us in Christ Jesus (1 John 4:7–12).

Jesus was full entering the wilderness, and he could face down the deepest questions of his personhood and identity because of that fullness of heart given to him by the Father. Can we experience that same fullness of heart as we go into our own wilderness experiences?

THE PRAYER

Lord of the Wild, there is an emptiness inside us that the loves of this world are eager to fill. They rush at us from every corner, saying they are the fountain we need. We want to love nothing more than you, Jesus, and for our loves to find their order in the context of your love for us and for your world. In Jesus's name, amen.

THE QUESTIONS

- Have you ever made yourself full of a love that was lesser than the love of God? What would it mean for you to welcome the Holy Spirit to speak into that love to help it find its proper place in the context of his love for you and for the entire world?

4

OF THE HOLY SPIRIT

LUKE 4:1

Jesus, full *of the Holy Spirit*, left the Jordan and was
led by the Spirit into the wilderness . . .

CONSIDER THIS

To be full of the Holy Spirit means we are full of the loving, manifest presence of God.

Who is the Holy Spirit, the one whom Jesus is full of as he goes away from the Jordan of his baptism?

The Holy Spirit is the presence of God; in fact, according to Genesis 1:2, the very energizing, life-giving breath of God. The Nicene Creed calls the Holy Spirit "the Lord, the giver of life." Jesus is full, satisfied, content with, sustained by the Holy Spirit as he goes into the wilderness.

I don't know about you, but I struggle with this. I have been satisfied by food. I have been satisfied by drink. I have been satisfied by relationships (in special moments), family laughter (in special moments), and even in vocational roles where I felt my calling was meeting, in some deep way, the needs of the world.

When one of my favorite authors, Frederick Buechner, wrote about vocation, he said:

> It comes from the Latin *vocare*, to call, and means the work a person is called to by God. There are all different kinds of voices calling you to all different kinds of work, and the problem is to find out which is the voice of God rather than of Society, say, or the Super-ego, or Self-Interest. By and large a good rule for finding out is this. The kind of work God usually calls you to is the kind of work (a) that you need most to do and (b) that the world most needs to have done. . . . *The place God calls you to is the place where your deep gladness and the world's deep hunger meet.*[6]

But this is important for us to say here, because it has tremendous pastoral implications for us as followers of Jesus.

In this baptism, Jesus received his business card: Beloved Son, pleasing to the Father before he even does one thing. But as Jesus is going into the wild where he will wrestle with the deepest questions of self-worth, purpose, and calling, the Bible does not say, "Jesus, full of satisfaction that he has a clear calling from God."

No. Jesus is not full of self-actualization, or even the gift of a clear word from the Father as to what he is to *do* with his life.

Jesus is full of the Holy Spirit, meaning he is full of the *loving, manifest presence of God.*

I believe this with all my heart: Jesus was so full of the Holy Spirit that even if he didn't do anything that we would call missional, or

---

6. Frederick Buechner, *Wishful Thinking: A Seeker's ABC* (New York: Harper & Row, 1993), 118–19, italics added.

ministry, or helpful to others, he would still have been full, satisfied, sustained by the presence of God. He was a beloved Son; that was his core vocation. At any given moment, he could have died—having fulfilled his calling.

Living in belovedness is fulfilling your calling, your vocation, in God. It will never be more complicated than that.

Have you ever thought you were right in the middle of your calling, what you might even call your vocation, and had whatever that platform was disappear in the blink of an eye? Maybe you were in a ministry role you felt good about, and perhaps even others respected you for your work. Then, a change happened, an unplanned circumstance came about, or someone made a decision that removed you from that role. Many Christians I know have gone into a tailspin at that point, so connected to their ministry that they practically fall away from God (and become mean to others) because their ministry disappeared. John Wimber, the founder of the Vineyard Movement of which I am a part, once said to this attitude (and I paraphrase), "You don't have a ministry. I don't have a ministry. We all have the ministry of Jesus."

When your name and Beloved Son or Beloved Daughter is all you have on your business card, then you are full of the Holy Spirit and ready to *do*, or *not to do*, anything that pleases the Father. God didn't call you or me to put a ministry on our spiritual business card. All he wants is our name on that card so he can say, "(insert your name), I need you here now," or "(insert your name), I need you here now, and not there," and we quickly obey. Whether we have a platform or not, we remain God's beloved child.

Jesus was full of the presence of God, the breath of God, going into the wild. We must be as well. Our vocation, our calling, is our sonship and daughterhood—not the tasks we do or the talents we have.

We must get this right. Jesus did; the biggest questions of calling in his heart had already been answered, and they had nothing to do with how impressive his résumé looked, or didn't look, at the time.

THE PRAYER

Lord of the Wild, our hearts are easily led to put our sense of self-worth and value in what we do to love and minister to others. We see now that until we have answered the belovedness question, with you, before we even step onto a field of ministry or service, we are vulnerable to the enemy confusing our calling. Our calling, our vocation, is to be your beloved child. Everything else, we are indifferent to. Use us as you will. In Jesus's name, amen.

THE QUESTIONS

- Have you ever put something on your spiritual business card, like a ministry or area of service, that you found your identity in? Was it ever taken away and, if so, how did you respond?

5

LEFT THE JORDAN

LUKE 4:1

Jesus, full of the Holy Spirit, *left the Jordan* and was
led by the Spirit into the wilderness . . .

CONSIDER THIS

Filled with the Spirit and covered by community, we must sometimes leave the familiar to face down the enemy—alone.

I like to think of the Jordan as the place of comfort, of ease, of familiarity and connection with others. The Jordan was a place of water, of crowds mutually agreeing on their need for repentance (from seeking other messiahs; that's what John the Baptist knew), and of provision. Jesus's dear cousin, John the Baptist, was being faithful and receiving him in the baptismal waters.

Would there have been deep friendship and comradery between them, sharing this "such a time as this" (see Est. 4:14) moment together in a way no one else (but Mary and Joseph) could ever understand? I think so.

The great German pastor and writer Dietrich Bonhoeffer—in his book on community, *Life Together*, written from a German prison cell—suggested that sometimes the psychological energy from being with a group of people can displace true trust in God for many. He suggested that we must learn to be alone with God, which is different from loneliness, for us to become whole and to not confuse the energies of friendship and community with intimacy with God.

Jesus had to leave the familiar, the warmth of companionship and the world in which he was known and named by others, to face down the enemy's challenges to his vocational call—his name in God. Jesus had to step away from being Mary's son, John's cousin, the best carpenter in his village (that's a fun guess), in order to become God's one and only Son—to inwardly affirm that call without others doing it for him.

In his baptism, it says that many heard the voice. John the Baptist surely did. But before they could pat him on the back, and get the discipleship party started, the Spirit led Jesus into the wild—the isolation of the wilderness.

Perhaps Jesus told this story, in part, for his disciples to understand why, as soon as everyone knew he was the Messiah, he disappeared for forty days.

Can you imagine many, including possibly John, asking: "Can I come with you, fast with you, as you apply this discipline of our faith and begin your ministry?"

If that did happen, I can imagine that Jesus would have said no with some degree of pain. He was beloved, yes. But he must have known the hard road that was ahead and would surely, as in the garden of Gethsemane, be encouraged by having a few friends with him as he faced the temptations of the enemy.

Who doesn't want moral support? Who doesn't need friends when the heart is most challenged to affirm our vocation, our calling, and to remind us who we are?

Jesus doesn't want it, that's who. Not at this moment. He knows it's time to be in the solitary place, the wild, the alone. He knows that much of his entire ministry would have to be self-motivated, Spirit-powered, and that the applause and encouragement of fickle disciples (remember Peter and the "Get behind me, Satan" moment in Matthew 16?) would get in his way.

Jesus must face his accuser *alone*.

He knows it won't be the last time. Gethsemane ahead, his baptism behind him, Jesus must leave the lush Jordan to enter the dry desert to face the one whose works he had come to destroy (1 John 3:8).

THE PRAYER

Lord of the Wild, we have often found more comfort in friends cheering us on than in your words of courage keeping us on track. Forgive us; we want to know your words of affirmation in that way that enables us to trust you even in complete isolation from others. We don't know what's ahead, but we want to find comfort in being alone with you, so when the moment of temptation comes, even from the well-meaning heart of a friend, we can stay the course. In Jesus's name, amen.

THE QUESTIONS

- Has the deep gift of friendship, of companionship, ever been a source through which you chose a path that you now realize was not the best choice for your relationship with God? How did you reset your relationship with God while still receiving the blessing and encouragement of your companions on the journey?

6

WAS LED BY THE SPIRIT

LUKE 4:1

Jesus, full of the Holy Spirit, left the Jordan and *was
led by the Spirit* into the wilderness . . .

CONSIDER THIS

The Spirit can lead us into seasons of testing, but always does so
for our good.

The wild is a place where Jesus, having lived for thirty years and
having been baptized and blessed by his Father, could have lost
everything.

Really? Everything? Perhaps that is too strong of a statement? And
we're talking about the Son of God here, right? The more I walk
with Jesus, learn about Jesus, and understand what it meant for
him to be the Son of God and the Son of Man, the more I believe
that if he truly faced every temptation that we do, but was without
sin (Heb. 4:15), then, yes, he could have lost everything.

Many people derail their entire lives (though never without the
possibility of healing and redemption) in a moment of choice,
giving in to a temptation they should have had the sense to avoid.
In a moment of choice, they forget their blessing, their name, their

calling as a child of God and their reason for living. People even take their lives in those moments of forgetting their name before God.

And this is where our theology of testing itself gets tested. Biblically, it is difficult to deny that God leads us into times of testing. Abraham was tested. Moses was tested. Jesus was tested and tempted. In the New Testament, we see these passages:

> In all this you greatly rejoice, though now for a little while you may have had to suffer grief in all kinds of trials. These have come so that the proven genuineness of your faith—of greater worth than gold, which perishes even though refined by fire—may result in praise, glory and honor when Jesus Christ is revealed. (1 Peter 1:6–7)

> Consider it pure joy, my brothers and sisters, whenever you face trials of many kinds, because you know that the testing of your faith produces perseverance. Let perseverance finish its work so that you may be mature and complete, not lacking anything. (James 1:2–4)

Yes, we say, but is God bringing us the tests, or is Satan, who also tests and tempts, doing that work? The book of Job makes it even more unclear: God notes his servant Job, Satan plots to tempt him, and God allows it to happen. In other words, testing comes; the Spirit may lead us to the testing, but isn't the one challenging us. As good friend and scholar Don Williams used to say, "The devil is God's devil." What he meant by that statement was that God works all things for the good (Rom. 8:28) when the devil challenges us—and in seeing the results of a child of God moving forward in obedience, the devil probably wishes he had never tried in the first place! He, in fact, made us stronger through the temptations!

Here we read that Jesus was "led by the Spirit" into the wild, put in a position where the enemy's temptations could have completely distorted Jesus's name and mission. And the Spirit of God leads him there. The word for *led* in this case means "brought," or "driven" by the Spirit. The word for *by*, in this case, can mean he was led in the Spirit or by the Spirit. Either way, the Spirit is somehow involved in this challenge to Jesus's vocation.

Is it surprising or unsettling that our faith must sometimes be tested to be proven genuine? That our faith gets refined through trial, and whether the Spirit initiated it or not, that our faith either becomes stronger or weaker as a result?

What Jesus had before him to do after the wilderness challenge reveals the weight of the entire world on his shoulders. He has been given his identity, "my Son," and it has come with affection and affirmation. After this will come his proclamation, his public ministry, his suffering, his death, and his commitment of his life into the Father's hands (Luke 23:46).

N. T. Wright puts it this way in referencing what happens after the desert:

> When Jesus said "the Spirit of the Lord is upon me," Luke has already let us into the secret. His years of silent preparation. His life of prayer leading up to his baptism. The confirmation of his vocation—and then its testing in the wilderness. Then, at last, going public with early deeds in Capernaum (as the exchange in the Nazareth synagogue makes clear, people had already heard of what he'd done elsewhere). Now, with years of prayer, thought and the study of scripture behind him, he stands before his own town. He knew everybody there and they knew him.[7]

---

7. N. T. Wright, *Luke for Everyone* (London: Society for Promoting Christian Knowledge and Westminster John Knox Press, 2001, 2004), 46–47.

The testing in the wild, led by the Spirit and carried out by the accuser and dismantler of people's identities before God, matters for Jesus's next steps in ministry—even in facing the derision of those in his hometown. Our own tests, in a similar way, matter for us. They put steel in our hearts. In our spiritual challenges, would it hurt to say, "The Spirit has led me here; do in me what you will, and may I be found faithful in this place," and then to resist the enemy who wants all the credit?

THE PRAYER

Lord of the Wild, there is testing in our own lives that simply looks like the temptation of the enemy. We choose to believe that you are with us in our trials, revealing faith in us and reinforcing our hearts for the next phase of life and ministry ahead. We will resist the enemy, and he will flee from us (James 4:7). But we will also look for you at work in our difficulties. In Jesus's name, amen.

THE QUESTIONS

- Have you faced a trial recently, or are you in one, that is revealing your strong and weak points of faith? Can you imagine that the Holy Spirit is involved in the process, showing you your own heart so you can be strengthened for greater challenges ahead?

7

INTO THE WILDERNESS

LUKE 4:1

Jesus, full of the Holy Spirit, left the Jordan and was
led by the Spirit *into the wilderness* . . .

CONSIDER THIS

Into the solitary place we must walk with Jesus to learn the art of
intimacy with God.

The Spirit led Jesus into the wilderness, sometimes translated "the
desert." For many, the word *desert* sounds hot, difficult, deadly, and
destructive. We think of deserts as having sand dunes, scorching
heat, and the worst part—no people, food, water, or corner stores.

But in the biblical narrative, the words *desert* and *wilderness*
are reflecting into Israel's forty-year journey in the wilderness,
wandering in covenant struggle with the God who brought them
up out of Egypt. The desert, the wilderness, was to be a place of
purification, of reorientation, of ongoing discovery of Israel's true
name and vocation. And they failed, time and time again, as a
people. In the wild, God can get at us—without the din and noise
and activity and relationships and social media creating enough
noise that we can't hear him speak what he has to say. The wild is
not a punishment—the wild is a *gift*.

Author John Mark Comer puts it this way:

> Desert here doesn't necessarily mean sand and heat. The Greek word is *eremos*, and it has a wide array of meanings. It can be translated desert, deserted place, desolate place, solitary place, lonely place, quiet place (my personal favorite), wilderness. There are stories—lots of them—in all four Gospels about Jesus' relationship to the *eremos*, but this is that first story.[8]

Jesus loved the eremos; some of his most important work was done there.

We see Jesus get up early to go into the quiet spaces. We see him looked for, and not found, because he is in a solitary place, and no one is with him. We see him invite his disciples into deserted places. We see Jesus choose early mornings and late nights to find alone time before the Father.

And there, in the wild, he reorients to his name and vocation time and time again.

The wild is a gift to you and to me. The pressures may be high in that place, or the pressures may be low. Either way, we need a place to stop, to think, to fast, to pray, to worship, and to confront the voice that has our worst in mind.

If we don't find the sacred place in the wild daily—the quiet, isolated, and present-with-God place—we will lose our way in the tame, the busy, the familiar, and the populated places. The Spirit led Jesus into the wilderness to set the tone for how he was to find his strength and solace to do the ministry ahead of him.

---

8. John Mark Comer, *The Ruthless Elimination of Hurry: How to Stay Emotionally Healthy and Spiritually Alive in the Chaos of the Modern World* (Colorado Springs, CO: Waterbrook, 2019), 123–24.

You and I must find our wild, our place of meeting, so we, too, can orient daily, weekly, monthly, and yearly, during our own disorienting lives.

Consider your wild place, where God can get you alone and you can hear his voice, reminding you of what is true, right, pure, lovely, and core to who you are. We won't find that kind of holy hearing happening in front of a Netflix series.

We will find it in the place of being alone before God.

THE PRAYER

Lord of the Wild, there are seasons in our lives that our idea of a bad time is being alone. We fear the loss of input, encouragement, resources, and even food and drink. But we recognize that you must be found in the quiet place so the noise can settle and reveal its true source (you or the enemy). We look forward to finding our quiet place together. In Jesus's name, amen.

THE QUESTIONS

- Do you have a daily or weekly quiet place where you can get before God and hear his voice? Have you set up a personal retreat by yourself, or with a group (we can hear God, at times, with others) this year? If not, would that be a good thing to do for your spiritual health?

8

WHERE

LUKE 4:1–2

Jesus, full of the Holy Spirit, left the Jordan and was led by the Spirit into the wilderness, *where* for forty days he was tempted by the devil. He ate nothing during those days, and at the end of them he was hungry.

CONSIDER THIS

God is a God of place—he meets with us in spaces and locations that become precious to our journey of intimacy and faith.

Where. Where are you right now? In your home? Your office? Sitting in your car? Is where you are a place where you meet with Jesus, or wrestle with your identity and pray through your problems?

The wild is where Jesus was led by the Spirit and encountered the fullness of the Spirit. The wild is also where Jesus fasted for forty days and was tempted by the devil.

The "where" of your encounter with God is often the same where of your battles with the enemy of your soul. In fact, I'm quite confident that the most important where of the story of Jesus in the wilderness is not the desert, the isolated place, itself. The where of the match we see in Luke 4 is on the same holy ground and battle grounds with which you and I are familiar—the where of the heart, the mind, and the body.

To my left, as I write this, is My Chair.

My Chair is a where in my journey with Christ. Each morning, early, I find my way to it. My journal and Bible are beside it, and I have a lap desk I pull out on which I read and write. Sometimes I sit in that chair, looking out the window, peacefully praying through the wonders and worries of the season of life I am in. I pray for my wife, my children, my family, my friends, and others whom the Lord has given me to pray for.

Another where for me is the driver's seat of My Truck. My Truck is a where in my journey with Christ. I spend much time in that seat each day, praying, worshipping, reflecting, and listening to the voice of the Father. Almost every Sunday, I take a long drive through the country near my home, talking to Jesus as one right there in the seat beside me. I speak. I listen. I wrestle. I deflect the bad.

The opposite is also true. My Chair is where the enemy tempts me to forget who I am, whose I am, and what I am for in this life. My Truck is also where the enemy tempts me to forget who I am, whose I am, and what I am for in this life. I wrestle, no matter how beloved I know I am, no matter how I have been blessed and affirmed and secured by the Father's love, with the enemy's voice. I believe that Jesus did too, and this was just the first outing in the confrontation of his life. (Peter's words to which Jesus said, "Get behind me, Satan," in Matthew 16:23, and the garden of Gethsemane, are just two other wheres we know about in the Gospels.)

I seek, in my where, to "Rejoice always, pray continually, give thanks in all circumstances; for this is God's will for you in Christ Jesus." I seek to "not quench the Spirit. Do not treat prophecies with contempt but test them all." I seek to "hold on to what is good," and "reject every kind of evil." In my where, I trust, like you, that "God himself, the God of peace," will "sanctify you through and through. May your whole spirit, soul and body be kept blameless at the coming of our Lord Jesus Christ. The one who calls you is faithful, and he will do it" (1 Thess. 5:16–24).

Because the blessings and the tests often coexist in those same spaces, I have found it incredibly important to make my wheres a haven for my meetings with Jesus—my faithful books before me, music ready to play, and instruments close at hand.

But the where we must worship, and the where we must win (needing encouragement from our community and bands along the way) is in the wild, the quiet place, the isolated place. When we win there, we can win anywhere—and the winning takes a lifetime.

THE PRAYER

Lord of the Wild, we can name the wheres, the places, where we worship, meet with you, and find your voice reminding us of our name. Often, in those same places, the battle rages in our minds, our hearts, and even in our bodies. Keep us focused on you, answering the voice of the enemy with your Word, just as you did in the desert. In Jesus's name, amen.

THE QUESTION

- Name the wheres that you meet with God. Have there been any recent victories where you felt your calling as a child of God and your purpose was contested, and you saw it through in that place?

9

FOR FORTY DAYS

LUKE 4:1–2

Jesus, full of the Holy Spirit, left the Jordan and was led by the Spirit into
the wilderness, where *for forty days* he was tempted by the devil. He
ate nothing during those days, and at the end of them he was hungry.

CONSIDER THIS

In forty days, Jesus did what Israel could not in forty years—he
resisted the temptation to exchange his identity for the promises
of the world.

God works with numbers. Not always, but often. Does the number
forty sound familiar to you in the Bible?

The number forty comes up a few times in the Scriptures, and
one of the most memorable is in the story of Israel, wandering for
forty years in the wilderness after leaving Egypt. The story of Jesus
in the wilderness for forty days—probably told by Jesus directly to
his disciples so that they would connect the dots with their people
Israel—is intimately connected to that covenant story in the Bible.

Let's recount it again, in summary. Israel, God's people, were led
out of Egypt under the guiding leadership of Moses and Aaron.
They saw God's work in a mighty deliverance through pestilence

and plagues. They saw miracles as they plundered the Egyptians (who willingly gave them their treasures), followed pillars of cloud and fire in their escape, and experienced the Red Sea parting before them and closing back on the Egyptian army.

Then, it happened. More disobedience. From grumbling to golden calves, the Israelites found every way possible to disbelieve God's vocation for them (to reveal his covenant love to the nations of the earth) and to retreat into their love of food, comfort, and even the arms of their oppressors (sounding familiar to the temptations of Jesus in our story?).

Israel failed to keep covenant *hesed*, loving-kindness, with Yahweh—though Yahweh kept his covenant with them.

Jesus will keep the covenant as a representative of his people Israel. He will embody their calling to the nations and will spread the good news they were intended to spread in the world, the Luke 4 calling to preach good news to the poor ("The Spirit of the Lord is on me" [Luke 4:18]).

Israel wandered in the wilderness of Sinai for forty years, forgetting the covenant name God had given them. A blessing on their identity, affection for his people, and affirmation of their value (see Jesus's baptism for the blessing the Israelites spurned as God's chosen family).

Jesus went into the wild for forty days, resisting the covenant-killer's taunts, full of the Holy Spirit and coming out victorious. Jesus did, in microcosm, what Israel could not do—keep covenant with Yahweh in their own season of testing.

While you and I don't need to mark forty days for enemy-resisting in our own lives—as we don't have the same mantle as Jesus—we can mark off times on the calendar as seasons for reorienting. In the Ignatian tradition (a spirituality with an openness to seeing God at work in all people, in all moments of life), many do retreats based on Ignatius's Spiritual Exercises for a similar time frame. Others write their own "rule of life," a code of personal values and spiritual practices that they will refer to again and again in their life of ministry.

What if we marked the calendar this year, even for just a long weekend or week, to meet with our Creator to renew our covenant relationship, resist the devil, and to come out oriented for the next season of our lives?

THE PRAYER

Lord of the Wild, thank you for leading the way in doing what Israel could not do, and modeling both covenant love and intentional practices of devotion in a season of being set apart. Guide us in our own planning of a shorter number of days for a yearly retreat or quarterly getaway to devote to remembering who we are in you. In Jesus's name, amen.

THE QUESTION

- If you took out your calendar now and planned a private retreat to get away and meet with Jesus, reaffirming your devotion to him, learning at his feet, and remembering who you are in him, where would you go and for how long?

10

HE WAS TEMPTED
BY THE DEVIL

LUKE 4:1–2

Jesus, full of the Holy Spirit, left the Jordan and was led by the Spirit into the wilderness, where for forty days *he was tempted by the devil*. He ate nothing during those days, and at the end of them he was hungry.

CONSIDER THIS

There is a spiritual power of evil that both exists and has a purpose—to get you to either forfeit or extinguish the precious gift of life your Creator has given you.

In the wilderness, Jesus contended with the devil not as one contends with an equal, but as one contends with a persistent distraction from vocation. You address it or you drift, you succumb, you lose faith in your own God-graced name. The path of life is taken, or the path of death (Ps. 16:11). That's the fight that is on.

In the Middle Ages, if you view art from that time period, you'll see the satan, meaning "accuser" or "adversary," depicted as a scaly, horned creature obviously bent on doing no good. This same kind of embodiment of satan, or "the satan" as the Hebrew suggests, continues to soften as history marches on. I think that's a good thing. Evil rarely presents itself as evil; it usually presents itself as a higher good.

The satan, as we reflect on the broader image of the devil passed down from ancient Hebrew tradition, is a spiritual presence that bends the heart toward wickedness. However we understand the satan (I'll keep that generic, lowercase name going just to keep the enemy in place and to counter the idea that satan is the opposite of God), there is a real demonic spirit of accusation and dehumanization alive in the world, a spiritual power that wars against the Creator's agenda and seeks to unseat the royal priesthood of God (you and I, according to 1 Peter 2:9) from our understanding of our place as a child of God and as the beloved of God.

In fact, that spiritual power is after *everyone* made in the image of God.

Almost immediately after Jesus was baptized in the waters of the Jordan, the Father and Spirit present, and almost as soon as Jesus received the belovedness blessing of his Abba and his clear vocational call as the Son of God, that vocation was *challenged*.

And we know our adversary does not play fair. In fact, one of the satan's primary ways of taking out beloved children of God, and those made in God's image, is to get us alone and then accuse us until we break and believe his evil, peppering, nagging, relentless, breath-stealing voice.

I've attended the funerals of those who have taken their life by suicide and walked with people through their stories of self-hatred before the Holy Spirit lifted them out of darkness into his marvelous light (1 Peter 2:9 again). No one can convince me there is not a spiritual power of evil focused on stealing, devouring, and destroying a soul this side of eternity. I've seen it, felt it, addressed it, and battled it myself. My guess is that you have, in some way, as well.

The satan, the accuser, knows the Lord who walked out of those baptismal waters. The satan knows that his mission is to "destroy the works of the evil one" (1 John 3:8). The satan knows that the life of the world is at stake. So, in the temptation that came with the testing in the wilderness, all bets were off, and the devil, as always, was pulling no punches. All of hell's fury was released at Jesus.

Friends and family, if you don't believe there is an enemy of your soul who is out to steal your life from you—one hateful thought, impression, narrative at a time—then you are being set up for a fall. Hell has one goal: to extinguish your life and end the possibility that you would find your hope in God.

Jesus confronted and defeated the satan in the wild. He held onto his belovedness and vocation. You and I can as well, because his Spirit lives within us. That's the way this works; the mystery of the gospel is Christ in us (Col. 1:27).

We conclude with 1 John 5:18–20a:

> We know that anyone born of God does not continue to sin; the One who was born of God keeps them safe, and the evil one cannot harm them. We know that we are children of God, and that the whole world is under the control of the evil one. We know also that the Son of God has come and has given us understanding, so that we may know him who is true.

Amen. To know Jesus is to know him who is true, and to distinguish his voice from him who is false.

Let's learn to know the difference.

Lord of the Wild, we know that voice that seeks to steal, kill, and destroy in our spirits. Help us to defeat the accuser, as Jesus did, with the Word of God in our hearts and the Spirit of God contending for us. In Jesus's name, amen.

THE QUESTIONS

- Have you ever seen a situation that was filled with evil righted by God and turned around for his glory? What was that like?

11

HE ATE NOTHING DURING THOSE DAYS

LUKE 4:1–2

Jesus, full of the Holy Spirit, left the Jordan and was led by the Spirit into the wilderness, where for forty days he was tempted by the devil. *He ate nothing during those days*, and at the end of them he was hungry.

CONSIDER THIS

To succeed on a spiritual battlefield for soul, we must go to the front lines with our appetites tamed, desperate and hungry for God.

If you knew you were going into the greatest challenge you would ever face to your calling and the fulfillment of your purpose on earth, how would you prepare? Would you keep your strength up? Go into a long season of mental and physical resilience training? Stock up on healthy food and drink resources to make sure your capacities would operate at their peak?

Or would you fast—*eating nothing*—for forty days?

Jesus understood that he would be at his peak reception to the Father's voice, and his greatest level of resistance to the enemy's voice, by fasting his way through the wild.

Fasting itself is a spiritual practice in which we say no to our desires, our appetites, and our tempting tastes so that we can yes to God's desires, God's will, and God's direction for our lives. Saying no to himself, Jesus was ready to say no to the enemy of the soul and the purposes of God.

Jesus was working his virtue muscles by fasting, telling his body that his spirit was full, and that was enough. It's not until we come to a full spirit being enough that we are truly ready to face down the offers of more that are inevitably there to tempt us.

Enough.

J. D. Walt says about fasting: "What if it takes seasons devoid of the temporal state of well-being we call happiness to truly know Joy? If so, a lot of us are well positioned to learn. These times that can try our souls have a way of emptying us out so something from beyond us can flood in. That is 'My Joy' according to Jesus. Come, Holy Spirit!"[9]

Fasting is a state of physical emptiness toward the goal of spiritual fullness. It is to resist the draw of food to enhance the draw of the food from heaven (John 4:32). Jesus knew that not putting food on his palate, chewing it, and then swallowing it was his path of preparation; his resistance to self-fulfillment was high, enabling him to stare down the enemy as even the grandest temptations came his way.

Fasting is a spiritual practice that, when done with healthy guidance and awareness by those who care for us medically, can open us to God in ways we can't on a full stomach. This may be a time to

---

9. J. D. Walt, Seedbed's 40-Day Fasting Challenge email, week 20.

fast for a meal or a day, to welcome the Holy Spirit to be our full-ness and our provision.

THE PRAYER

Lord of the Wild, resisting our own desires is not something we are well practiced in, but we understand how it helps build resilience in us to say no to the enemy's offers of fulfillment. Teach us to fast in a way that works for us, and that leads us into deeper intimacy with you—the Bread of Heaven. In Jesus's name, amen.

THE QUESTIONS

- Have you ever fasted before? If so, how do you think it helped you spiritually in that season of your life?

12

AND AT THE END OF THEM HE WAS HUNGRY

LUKE 4:1–2

Jesus, full of the Holy Spirit, left the Jordan and was led by the Spirit into the wilderness, where for forty days he was tempted by the devil. He ate nothing during those days, *and at the end of them he was hungry*.

CONSIDER THIS

Like you and me, Jesus knew what it meant to be hungry for food, thirsty for water, and strengthened by friendship.

Jesus, in the wild, is a real person with real needs. Lest we think for a moment that Jesus was supernaturally better than we are at facing trials and temptations, this little verse is there for our benefit. After fasting for forty days, the Bible wants us to know that Jesus was *hungry*.

The implication here is that Jesus is like us, and after fasting for forty days, he had needs. His stomach wanted refreshment. His body wanted sustenance. His palate wanted to taste good food (and to bless God for it). Jesus most certainly had his favorite foods, just as you or I would.

I've had bread in Israel. And some of that freshly baked bread just melted in my mouth. I was hungry when I had it, and I was deeply satisfied once I had a few bites.

The enemy will not come at us, aiming at our points of strength. He will always be aiming at our points of weakness. For Jesus, it was hunger for food—especially good food.

I love this quote from J. D. Walt on why fasting can reorient us in times when our appetites are leading us along:

> We live in an age and in a land where, practically speaking, our god is our stomach. I am convicted deeply by this even as I write it. If I'm honest, I must confess that I feed my stomach far more than I feed my relationship with God. And here's the mystery—fasting from what feeds my stomach has the effect of feeding my relationship with God. Let's focus our fasting as an offering of our appetites to God. We can try and try to curb our appetites and fail. So what if we just offered our appetites to God through the act of fasting and see what he can do with them?[10]

The devil was about to speak to Jesus. As for us, the devil would speak to Jesus in the language of desire, of want, even need. Jesus had mastered his hunger and thirst, and his appetite for the basics we all take for granted every day. Augustine noted that our desires are what make us who we are. As James K. A. Smith put it: "You are what you love."[11]

---

10. Walt, 40-Day Fasting Challenge, week 5.

11. James K. A. Smith, *You Are What You Love: The Spiritual Power of Habit* (Grand Rapids, MI: Brazos Press, 2016), 10.

Jesus denied himself food in order to reorder his loves and align them to his will—the Father's will. He subjugated his bodily desires to his will—the Father's will.

In fasting, the Spirit helps us train ourselves to offer even our appetites and desires as an offering of worship to our Savior. Like Jesus, the practice of fasting can lead us into deep places of intimacy with God if we will do so in obedience and with wisdom.

Jesus was hungry. Being in need does not mean we are outside of God's perfect will. In fact, as Jesus demonstrated, being in need can mean we are right in the center of our best life with God.

In Philippians 4:19 we read: "And my God will meet all your needs according to the riches of his glory in Christ Jesus." Can we trust God to meet our needs, and can we practice not being so controlled by our basic needs by practicing fasting?

THE PRAYER

Lord of the Wild, you demonstrated how fasting can orient us to the Father's will and help us to align and order our desires according to a higher purpose. Give us the wisdom to know how and when to practice overcoming our will related to our basic desires. Train us to yield our will to yours and draw us closer to your heart in the process. In Jesus's name, amen.

THE QUESTIONS

- Have you ever fasted before? If so, was it a meaningful experience?

13

THE DEVIL SAID TO HIM

LUKE 4:1–3

Jesus, full of the Holy Spirit, left the Jordan and was led by the Spirit into the wilderness, where for forty days he was tempted by the devil. He ate nothing during those days, and at the end of them he was hungry.

The devil said to him, "If you are the Son of God, tell this stone to become bread."

CONSIDER THIS

The accuser, the satan, has words for Jesus. As we know, "the tongue has the power of life and death, and those who love it will eat its fruit" (Prov. 18:21). The Word made flesh is about to be addressed, with words, by the supreme liar of the universe.

It is important to note here that many scholars believe that Jesus was not speaking to a physical manifestation of the devil (like medieval images might suggest), but rather to the enemy of our souls who speaks to us—including you and me—through thoughts that enter our heads and impressions that create fear, anxiety, distress, and demonic experiences for each one of us.

New Testament scholar N. T. Wright puts it this way: "The story does not envisage Jesus engaged in conversation with a visible figure to whom he could talk as one to another; the devil's voice appears as a string of natural ideas in his own head. They are plausible, attractive, and make, as we would say, a lot of sense."[12] In other words, the devil was speaking to Jesus in the same way the devil speaks to us—in ways that make us think we ourselves are coming up with the ideas being planted.

This is not to diminish the reality of the evil spirit, the devil, in any way. It is rather to suggest that our images of an ugly little creature on our shoulder, or appearing in a dark corner to tempt us, may be far less biblical than simply traditional interpretations carried to us by paintings and images from extrabiblical sources.

In my own journey, connected to some painful experiences in my childhood, I have experienced seasons of overtly demonic dreams. I have also experienced moments of profound deliverance, and my dreams have been affected in a positive way.

To ignore the devil as the source of the voice that encourages us to forget who and whose we are, to want to act out in unholy anger, retain bitterness, entertain shame, shame others, and even to take our own precious lives (or regard ourselves as useless), is to welcome our own destruction.

The satan, the adversary, spoke to Jesus. And Jesus spoke back, using the written Word of God as his answers. This leads us to an important insight for us. Jesus chose to use the Word of God, hidden in his heart for such a time as this, to respond to the attacking words of the enemy.

The importance of memorizing, meditating on, and hiding the Word of God in our hearts cannot be overstated—you will need

---

12. N. T. Wright, *Luke for Everyone*, 43.

DAN WILT

it during a battle for your heart yet to come. I have had moments when I was at the very end of my rope, wanting to give up completely and to check myself into an institution. Perhaps you have had similar "end of yourself" moments. In those times, sometimes in the middle of a dark night of the soul, the Word of God has been on my tongue and has been the right, powerful word to silence the voice of the evil one.

Jesus had the same enemy we do, and the stakes were high in the wild for Jesus—and for us. Know that the enemy has something to say about your life and will manipulate your thoughts and feelings to get his evil point across: that you are worthless and unloved.

Nothing could be farther from the truth. Any voice that speaks to you and tells you that you are worthless is hideously demonic at the root—and is the opposite of the loving blessing the Father speaks over your life.

Like Jesus, let's answer with the enduring Word of God when the devil speaks.

THE PRAYER

Lord of the Wild, we realize that there is a battle raging all around us, and the enemy of our soul is planning to devour us—often doing so with words spoken into our minds and hearts. We recognize the presence and work of the enemy and address that evil voice that we might move forward in freedom in you. In Jesus's name, amen.

- Have you ever experienced a voice in your head or heart, or even through another person, that was dehumanizing and devaluing? How did you address it, and did you come out believing God's Word over the word of the devil?

14

IF (PART ONE)

LUKE 4:1–3

Jesus, full of the Holy Spirit, left the Jordan and was led by the Spirit into the wilderness, where for forty days he was tempted by the devil. He ate nothing during those days, and at the end of them he was hungry.

The devil said to him, "*If* you are the Son of God, tell this stone to become bread."

CONSIDER THIS

Your calling will be contested; you must learn to identify the little words that call it into question.

If.

What a powerful, little word. It is only two letters long, but the very mention of it can dissolve the courage of the greatest saint. "If" you are really who you say you are, "then" things would or should be different.

While the devil is tempting Jesus, it is also clear that, like Israel before him, Jesus is facing a test—and the Spirit has led him into it. This can make us uncomfortable, but the implication is right here in our text. Israel was tested in the wilderness, and Jesus is tested as well.

As N. T. Wright explains: "Luke has just reminded us of Jesus' membership in the family of Adam. If there had been any doubt about his being really human, Luke underlines his sharing of our flesh and blood in this vivid scene of temptation."[13] In other words, Jesus is of the family of Adam, and the enemy is approaching him the way he would any other human—only knowing the stakes are much, much higher.

And how does the enemy approach you and me? Often with "if/then" statements, woven into our minds as though they are our own thoughts and clear perceptions of reality. In the wild with Jesus, the word "if" is used *three times* by the devil, for one purpose—to unsettle and uproot the name and vocation given to Jesus in his baptismal waters.

If.

Every day, we hear some version of that word dancing in our own heads, putting a question mark between us and our blessing as the beloved of God—often to get us inwardly deciding once again if God is good, if we are precious, if we matter, and if we will ever find joy in this life.

If.

We must master the implications of this word so that, when it arrives in our mind like a lightning bolt on a stormy evening, we can deflect its power in our weakest and most insecure moments.

Like Jesus, when the enemy speaks an "if" word to you, and your internal answer leaves you feeling lost and without hope in the

---

13. N. T. Wright, *Luke for Everyone*, 42.

world, then you know it is not an if from the Lord (like, "If my people, who are called by my name, will humble themselves and pray" from 2 Chronicles 7:14).

And every "if" implies a "then," even if it's not explicit in the sentence. We compare ourselves to ourselves-as-we-dream-of-being, and to others, and we despair. "If" we were really this, "then" that would happen. "If" God is in us, "then" why am I struggling with anxiety and mental health issues?

We struggle because we have not found our identity and vocation in the Father's blessing as Jesus did; we listen to that if/then statement. Here's a new one: "If" God loves you, "then" God loves you. Let's hold on to that one when the clouds come rolling in.

If/then statements are called "conditional statements" in grammar for a reason; they are statements that cause us to consider our conditions and their outcome. Master the "if" coming at your own life right now and learn to discern from where it is emanating. When it's coming from the enemy, and pride or despair begins to spike in your heart, see it for what it is—a word from the devil—and refuse its unsettling of your trust in your heavenly Father, or yourself, as you walk with Christ.

THE PRAYER

Lord of the Wild, teach us to discern between when you are calling us to compare ourselves to a higher goal, and that comparison is accompanied by hope, and when the enemy is taunting us to compare ourselves to a proud or fearful dream in our hearts. In Jesus's name, amen.

THE QUESTIONS

- Say, "If God loves me, then God loves me" a few times over. What else could you do today to remind yourself that if/then statements that bring a sense of despair or fear are from the enemy? How will you respond when it happens?

15

YOU ARE THE SON OF GOD

LUKE 4:1–3

Jesus, full of the Holy Spirit, left the Jordan and was led by the Spirit into the wilderness, where for forty days he was tempted by the devil. He ate nothing during those days, and at the end of them he was hungry.

The devil said to him, "If *you are the Son of God*, tell this stone to become bread."

CONSIDER THIS

Jesus already had his identity questions answered—and he didn't need the devil or a crowd to affirm it. He knew who he was.

What does it mean that Jesus is the Son of God, and what does that have to do with us living in the fullness of our own vocation—our own calling—in God?

In the baptismal waters of Luke 3, Jesus is named by the Father. "This is my Son." There is no gray area here, no "sort of" or "possibly" statements to diminish the impact of the words.

Jesus is the Son of God. He knows he is the Son of Man. He grew up like the rest of us did. But Son of God? It has just been doubly, triply confirmed in his baptism, before his ministry has begun.

"Son" is the title the Father gave him, reminded him of, held out for all to hear.

Now, in this verse of Luke 4, that is the very title that the devil goes after with an if/then statement.

The first goal of the enemy is to put a question mark where there was a period inside of Jesus. See it this way from the enemy: "Son of God?" Our inner spiritual punctuation matters. In this case, though the devil words the sentence differently, an unspoken question mark is following his title of Jesus.

"If you are the Son of God."

It's like the devil was saying, "If you are the Son of God (and I wonder how you could really think you are given that you are hungry, thirsty, hot, sweaty, about to be hated, and on the outside of civilization), then tell . . ."

There is a second important idea going on here. The embodiment of evil is giving Jesus a *command*. If the Son of God does what the devil wants and deigns to fulfill the suggestion, then another quiet battle is won for darkness. It would mean the Son of God capitulated to the request, the suggestion, the "bright" idea of the prince of darkness.

It's a power game. I question your identity as soon as you receive it, and I get you, subtly, to do my will in one small increment. That's the perfect recipe for eventual enslavement.

Jesus will have none of it. He knows that the Father has named him "My Son"—and he is not about to let the enemy erase it from his business card with a question mark and a suggestion he make bread.

Jesus already had his identity question answered—and he didn't need the devil or a crowd to affirm it. He knew who he was. No crowd would court his favor from that point on; he had no one to impress and everyone to save.

The Lord has called you and me by name. We have identity in the Father, and just as we are reveling in our belovedness and favor with God, the enemy is right there to try to steal our identity from us. Daily. Know who you are, reaffirm it in prayer, spiritual practices, and mental habits—and don't waver from your identity.

You are a child of God. It's on your spiritual business card. The enemy will challenge that identity, that well-defined role and vocation (yes, being a covenant child of God is your and my primary calling in life) right out of the gate through which it was just affirmed.

Jesus didn't need the enemy to affirm his Sonship; nor did he need any crowd to do the same. "Son of God," for Jesus, was followed by the punctuation mark of a period. It was a done deal. The enemy's question mark had no soft place to land.

THE PRAYER

Lord of the Wild, we have a name you've given us, and we're not about to sacrifice it when the enemy repeats it back to us with a question mark. We trust in what you've said about our sonship or daughterhood over any voice that sells us an alternate identity. In Jesus's name, amen.

THE QUESTIONS

- Do the enemy's taunts about your identity in Christ have a soft landing place, a welcome hooking spot? What could you do to change that?

16

TELL THIS STONE TO BECOME BREAD

LUKE 4:1–3

Jesus, full of the Holy Spirit, left the Jordan and was led by the Spirit into the wilderness, where for forty days he was tempted by the devil. He ate nothing during those days, and at the end of them he was hungry.

The devil said to him, "If you are the Son of God, *tell this stone to become bread.*"

CONSIDER THIS

Let's sit, for a moment, on the verb *tell*. It is a Greek word that also means "command." The devil is telling Jesus to command something, to use his power to meet a personal need.

And this is how the three temptations, which reflect the broader test behind this all, begin. Jesus, use your power, presence, and prestige for personal gain.

There it is: yield cruciform love for others to the inward desire to be known and loved by all. Yield suffering for gain. Yield your name as the beloved Son of God! Yield the name Jesus, "the Lord saves." Save yourself! Preserve yourself! Let the world suffer while you sip a margarita.

Look around at all the margarita sippers with wealth and power who deign to help alleviate some suffering in the world, but rarely to the point of their own suffering. Giving, the kind that breaks chains, will always cost us something. Our skin will be in the game; our blood will be in the battle. That is cruciformity; that is entering into the pain and becoming one with that pain in order to truly break its shackles.

This first temptation is not about bread. It is about power and its misdirection. Every abuse of power we have ever seen in the world—from the power to choose in the garden to the powers that war against the Lord and his Anointed One in Revelation—is rooted in this temptation.

The enemy of your soul and mine is after our power, our agency to act. If he can't remove it completely, making us feel powerless and falling into utter despair, then he will get us to misdirect and abuse others for our own benefit.

Power used in the ultimate service of self affirms the enemy's grip on our lives. We can enjoy what God has given us, yes. But we cannot focus on keeping ourselves from suffering with the world by using our power to gain lordship over others. We cannot simply use our power for personal gain.

Our examples of benevolence, even our most noble uses of personal agency, are too weak to stand alongside cruciform love in action. Benevolence is helping someone with my overflow, applying my goodwill and resources to their better fortune.

But what if a friend has no extended family resources to receive any inheritance on either side of their family? What if jobs and saving has been a grueling struggle, exacerbated by a pandemic, and the person has a strong work ethic but lacks the natural or spiritual gift of generating money? What if their place in society fed that lack and they will experience great challenges when they are seventy years old and struggle to work?

Where, then, is our agency to act with cruciformity, and how will we act in the world?

It is in the hard and troubling moments that we must choose our path with our time, our energies, and our resources. We only have one life to live, and we choose to live it in the way of Jesus.

Jesus had the power to turn that stone into bread. He chose not to. He's about to say why. But, for the moment, Jesus is acting with cruciformity in his character set—and that virtue will set the path for his saving work among us.

THE PRAYER

Lord of the Wild, we have agency to act on our behalf, on behalf of those we love, and on behalf of those to whom you send us. Help us to discern how to use the power that runs through our hands and influence. Teach us the way of love, that the power we have might find its roots in the greater, contextualizing power of love. In Jesus's name, amen.

THE QUESTIONS

- Is there an area of your life where you have the ability to guide circumstances, and you are choosing to act in love with that power or resource you've been given? What has been the result?

17

JESUS ANSWERED (PART ONE)

LUKE 4:1–4

Jesus, full of the Holy Spirit, left the Jordan and was led by the Spirit into the wilderness, where for forty days he was tempted by the devil. He ate nothing during those days, and at the end of them he was hungry.

The devil said to him, "If you are the Son of God, tell this stone to become bread."

Jesus answered, "It is written: 'Man shall not live on bread alone.'"

CONSIDER THIS

If we don't address temptation directly, firmly, and with Christ-honoring resolve—we will succumb to the evil one's false promises again and again.

In a world of reaction, alarm, and shock, a population reacting to all manner of news and offenses, we read that Jesus *responded* to the devil. In this passage, Jesus is not reacting, controlled by the devil's play—he has chosen to answer the devil on his own terms.

When the devil goes unanswered, avoided, or dismissed, he comes back around again with the same question.

Here we have our role model for speaking to the enemy. Jesus doesn't engage the conversation, mind you. Rather, he provides a clear and soul-born direct answer to the taunt behind the enemy's temptation.

"Follow my guidance, Jesus; use your power for your own good" is my paraphrase of the satan's suggestion.

"Bread, even though I am hungry, is not what I need. I need to learn to use the power I've been given for the sake of others" is my paraphrase of Jesus's answer.

This is where we lose some human contact with Jesus. When I have a need, and I have the power to fill it, I do. There is no question. There is no pause. My body is hungry and my mouth is watering. I feed it. No harm in that, eh? Anyone want to fault me? No. We all do it.

But for Jesus, there is harm in that, in this moment. He is not in the wild to answer to his body and its cravings. He is in the wild to learn to act from his vocational center—as the Son of God who came into the world not to be served, but to serve and to give his life for the sake of many (Matt. 20:28).

Sometimes our needs and our response to them get smack in the way of the training of the heart that Paul spoke of in 1 Corinthians 9:25–26. We are after a crown that will last forever, after a life of love that will feed the masses; bread is not on the menu tonight for Jesus, or for us.

Jesus is practicing for the cross from this first temptation on. The internal spiritual muscles of his calling, his virtue set, are being flexed. How does he resist such a basic suggestion, meeting such a core need no one would fault him for?

He answers the seemingly innocent, yet insidious suggestion. He disempowers it at the source-level, in his heart, and he disempowers the devil from asking it again. His resolve is fire, and his spoken, Word-saturated answer will consume the question both for the vocation-unseater and for himself. He will not look back. His power is not for his own gratification.

Jesus, be the role model for every one of us and the agency we have been given in this life. Let us use it, with cruciformity and from the foundation of love, for the sake of others.

THE PRAYER

Lord of the Wild, our track record for obedience is less than flawless, but our desire to use our gifts and privileges in ways that honor you and serve others is passionate. Teach us cruciform love; it is the highest love we seek. In Jesus's name, amen.

THE QUESTIONS

- Has there been something you've recently given up to be faithful to Jesus that others might say you don't need to give up? What was it, and what do you think the result of your obedience will be?

18

IT IS WRITTEN (PART ONE)

LUKE 4:1–4

Jesus, full of the Holy Spirit, left the Jordan and was led by the Spirit into the wilderness, where for forty days he was tempted by the devil. He ate nothing during those days, and at the end of them he was hungry.

The devil said to him, "If you are the Son of God, tell this stone to become bread."

Jesus answered, "*It is written*: 'Man shall not live on bread alone.'"

CONSIDER THIS

Have you ever hidden a verse from the Scriptures in your heart, and when all hell was breaking loose, repeated it until you entered its truth and believed it once again?

When Adam and Eve stumbled in the garden, it was because they did not have an answer for the enemy. Their hearts failed them. They did what Israel did, time and time again. They did what Jesus would not; they failed to answer their enemy.

"It is written" is a phrase that I want to become accustomed to, within my own mind, and in my outward answers to situations and temptations that arise.

There is a better Word than our own to answer the enemy with. Jesus reaches for it. He reaches deep into the covenant narrative of his people for it. In using the phrase, he is invoking an entire history of God's faithfulness and a spectacular tapestry of worship gone right.

"It is written" is a great way for you and me to answer the enemy when the whispers come.

Several years ago, I went through a very dark season of an entire year battling with health issues, mental health struggles, and a lingering and choking insomnia. In the middle of the night one evening, one in which I thought I might lose my mind, I hit the wall. My face was in a pillow as I knelt on the cold floor, and the chasm between my loving Father and me felt impassable. I was ready to wake my wife to take me to the hospital to check me in. It was a no-turning-back, life-or-death moment in my spirit.

Then, the Word of God came to mind: "Your word gives me life" (Ps. 119:50 NCB). I repeated the phrase over and over into that pillow, so the sound was muffled, and I didn't wake my wife. At first, I yelled it. Then, as I repeated it, my voice became lower until I entered a slight peace that steadied me.

In those moments, the enemy had almost convinced me I would lose my mind, and that my life and my relationships would fall utterly apart. My answers, my emotionally fragmented and best-sourced answers, even those from positive-thinking quotes and inspired authors, fell flat.

The enemy was winning. I had to have an answer for him that would confront his slow erosion of my sense of calling to be a beloved child of God. He told me God was not good, or that I would be much healthier and stable than I was. He suggested that if "he grants sleep to those he loves" (Ps. 127:2), I must not be one of those he loves.

I felt my heart beginning to move toward hatred of my life in all its misery, and even toward hatred of God for not delivering me from my mental anguish—and that's when the Word of God, hidden in my heart, reared up and gave me an answer to give.

You know when, in soccer (which I hope you love as my family does), a goal is scored after one scored by the rival team and the announcer lifts his or her voice? I love the moment when the announcer says, "And (my team) *answers* with a goal—to win the game!"

I want to answer the enemy, in my darkest moments, with a goal-scoring Word that is better than my own good shot or pass. I want a Word to go in the net, to rip it, to stun my rival, and to end the game. It is to the written Word of God we must go in those moments, just as Jesus did.

When we use the Word of God to answer the enemy, we invoke thousands of years of covenant love and faithful lives in the process. With the Word of God in our hearts and on our lips—spoken, sung, or screamed into a pillow—we can win our battles.

"It is written."

The net is ripped clean through. The game is over. Thanks for coming.

THE PRAYER

Lord of the Wild, your Word is a living and active, double-edged sword (Heb. 4:12), and is the sword of the Spirit

(Eph. 6:17). Teach us to answer the enemy with, "It is written," rather than struggling for words born of our own strength and will. In Jesus's name, amen.

THE QUESTIONS

- Is there a verse you would call your life verse or a go-to verse that you draw on in your darkest moments? What is it, and what does it mean to you?

19

MAN SHALL NOT LIVE ON BREAD ALONE

LUKE 4:1–4

Jesus, full of the Holy Spirit, left the Jordan and was led by the Spirit into the wilderness, where for forty days he was tempted by the devil. He ate nothing during those days, and at the end of them he was hungry.

The devil said to him, "If you are the Son of God, tell this stone to become bread."

Jesus answered, "It is written: '*Man shall not live on bread alone.*'"

CONSIDER THIS

What good thing do you need to resist to embrace God's best?

The human heart is made for more than surviving; it is made for thriving. As we look at Jesus's answer to the first temptation, and the others that follow, some background is in order.

Forty days in the wild for Jesus; forty years in the wild for Israel. Forty days in the wild for Jesus to pass his test of vocation and purpose as the *Son of God*. Forty years for Israel to struggle and fail, wander and wish, stumble and fall—ultimately failing to pass their test and affirm their vocation and purpose to share the covenant love of Yahweh with the world as a nation of priests, as the *People of God* (Ex. 19:3–6).

The three temptations (tests) that form the heart of the narrative take us deep into the book of Deuteronomy—and the millennia-ancient covenant story of God and Israel.

Jesus's answers to the temptations of the satan quote from Deuteronomy directly, and tie us back to the truth that Jesus's story is integrally connected to Israel's story—and vice versa.

To the first temptation to a) obey the devil's suggestion, and b) turn a stone into some hot, buttery, gap-filling, hunger-satiating bread, Jesus answers: "It is written: 'Man shall not live on bread alone.'"

Jesus is answering the pressure of the enemy to misuse his agency and power (it's the same temptation that the snake used on Adam and Eve in the garden, and the same used on Israel and humans for all time after) for his own benefit.

He quotes from the powerful passage in Deuteronomy 8:1–5 (emphasis mine), in a sense, on behalf of all of us:

> Be careful to follow every command I am giving you today, so that you may live and increase and may enter and possess the land the LORD promised on oath to your ancestors. Remember how the LORD your *God led you all the way in the wilderness these forty years, to humble and test you in order to know what was in your heart,* whether or not you would keep his commands. He humbled you, causing you to hunger and then feeding you with manna, which neither you nor your ancestors had known, to teach you that *man does not live on bread alone but on every word that comes from the mouth of the LORD.* Your clothes did not wear out and your feet did not swell during these

forty years. Know then in your heart that as a man disciplines his son, so the LORD your God disciplines you.

Jesus's covenant-powered answer is from this culminating moment in the first books of Deuteronomy. Let's summarize the backstory that leads to it.

In Deuteronomy 1, Moses is with God's people in the wilderness (and they are "a heavy burden," verse 9).

In Deuteronomy 2, they continue their forty years of wandering (and they have "not lacked anything," verse 7).

In Deuteronomy 3, they are about to take possession of the land by crossing the Jordan (and Moses will not be allowed to go in, verse 26).

In Deuteronomy 4, Israel is called to obedience and to avoid idolatry (that they might "know that the LORD is God, and there is no other," verse 35).

In Deuteronomy 5, they are given the Ten Commandments with a call to obedience (that they may "live and prosper" over long days, verse 33).

In Deuteronomy 6 we read the great Shema of Israel and the call to love in covenant with Yahweh ("Hear, O Israel: The LORD our God, the LORD is one. Love the LORD your God with all your heart and with all your soul and with all your strength. These commandments that I give you today are to be on your hearts," verses 4–6).

In Deuteronomy 7, Yahweh affirms both his covenant affection and covenant faithfulness to Israel (one could almost weep during the chapter reading, about this small, chosen people, and how "the LORD loved you and kept the oath," verses 7–9).

In Deuteronomy 8, and Jesus's answering of the devil from it, Jesus is essentially saying, "My covenant is not with you, Accuser and Un-Namer of Adam and Eve, Israel, God's historic people, and me—it is with my Father." Manna is not the bread of life. The Word of Yahweh is—and Jesus is the very Bread of Life standing before the most evil of spirits, resisting his feeble offer. Jesus resisted the bread to become the Bread of Life—for us all (John 6:35).

He doesn't have time for party games and quick desire fixes with his adversary. He has come to undo the works of that very evil one—it is his central mission and Son of God purpose (1 John 3:8).

As followers of Jesus, it is *our* mission as well.

THE PRAYER

Lord of the Wild, we are free because you answered the satan in this first temptation to use your power for yourself. You used it for us. To free us. To feed us on the Bread of Life, you and your transforming, awakening, covenant love. You have filled us with all we need; we choose to give the enemy no quarter in our own dealings with his un-naming, disorienting voice. We choose your way, and we will answer the enemy with the Word as well. In Jesus's name, amen.

THE QUESTION

- What does it mean to you that Jesus is the Bread of Life (John 6:35)?

20

THE DEVIL LED HIM

LUKE 4:1–5

Jesus, full of the Holy Spirit, left the Jordan and was led by the Spirit into the wilderness, where for forty days he was tempted by the devil. He ate nothing during those days, and at the end of them he was hungry.

The devil said to him, "If you are the Son of God, tell this stone to become bread."

Jesus answered, "It is written: 'Man shall not live on bread alone.'"

The devil led him up to a high place and showed him in an instant all the kingdoms of the world.

CONSIDER THIS

Jesus allowed the devil to lead him places, only because the Spirit first led him there. It was the work of holy sabotage at its best.

Does today's phrase sound familiar, yet strange?

In Luke 4:1, we read that the Spirit "led" Jesus into the wild. Now we read that the "devil led" Jesus to a high place (v. 5). Here we are, pausing in our journey to realize that *Jesus allowed the devil to lead him somewhere.*

And so, the second temptation begins.

This is where I think Jesus and we are radically different. Even allowing ourselves to entertain a vision from the enemy can be fatal for us.

Many years ago, I was on a cliff's edge in New Zealand. It was the highest cliff in the country. I was afraid to go to the edge, feeling the expanse would suck me toward it. My good friend looked at me, shook his head, and said, "Why don't you crawl to the edge?" He wanted me to have the view, but safely. I laid flat on my face, crawling to the edge (and he held my ankles for good measure). I was glad I got the view, but thankful I did so on my face with a physical demonstration of humility keeping me grounded.

When we stand on an edge, proud and confident, there is always a wind waiting to push us over. Think about all the celebrities who walk tall to the edges, pushing boundaries not only of their art form, but also of morality, character, and achievement.

As Denzel Washington famously said in recent times, "At your highest moment, be careful, that's when the devil comes for you." Many celebrities have fallen, I believe, because deep within them is a creed that tells them they can ultimately control the wind as they stand high on the edge. They're not necessarily explicitly unbelievers; they are just as firmly believers in themselves as they are in God.

The Father will not compete with anyone or anything; even one's positive self-esteem.

Humility is expressed in more than words and attitudes; it is an inner state of the heart that must be cultivated and nurtured through continual acts of humbling oneself, even in the face of glistening opportunity and wild success. "Humility," it has been said, "is not too high a view of ourselves or too low—it is an accurate view of ourselves." We are tested in these moments, when things are going right. If we begin to believe our own reviews, we can lose our way.

Pride comes before a fall (Prov. 16:18); this is the moment Jesus has been led to by the devil.

The devil, otherwise known as the traitor and slanderer, will lead you places. You won't even know you are standing on a height, because the way will seem so normal, so the result of your faithfulness and goodness, so the result of your gifts and good choices.

"Make a name for yourself" was the old encouragement from parents and grandparents and people invested in your reputation. While well-meaning, that sounds exactly like the devil in sheep's (or relative's) clothing. We are not here to make much of ourselves. Jesus knew that, even being the Son of God. He was here to make much of his Father. We are here to make much of Jesus. The Holy Spirit is here to glorify the Father and the Son. And the name-serving continues.

The devil wants you to make a name for yourself, to operate in your gifts for the satisfaction of yourself. That's what he was doing with Jesus in the second temptation.

But nonetheless, the devil may lead you there, hoping for an "opportune" moment (Luke 4:13) to give you one little push—into losing your God-given name and replacing it, quietly in your heart, with the name you have made for yourself. You may be led to a high place many times in your life; the key is to walk away before you make that kingdom your own.

THE PRAYER

Lord of the Wild, we are tempted to make a name for ourselves, and in so desiring it, we have allowed the devil to lead us to high places where we thought we were seeing our future kingdom rather than yours. Meet us in the place in our hearts that craves validation and honor for our name, experience, and skills. Address the wound that makes us vulnerable to the enemy in this temptation and heal us. In Jesus's name, amen.

THE QUESTION

- Be honest with yourself today. Think of the last time you were applauded for your gifts and application of help to another. Were you able to receive the compliment with grace and humility, did you deflect it as if you deserved no thanks, or did you take a bit too much pleasure in having your name recognized?

21

UP TO A HIGH PLACE

LUKE 4:1–5

Jesus, full of the Holy Spirit, left the Jordan and was led by the Spirit into the wilderness, where for forty days he was tempted by the devil. He ate nothing during those days, and at the end of them he was hungry.

The devil said to him, "If you are the Son of God, tell this stone to become bread."

Jesus answered, "It is written: 'Man shall not live on bread alone.'"

The devil led him **up to a high place** and showed him in an instant all the kingdoms of the world.

CONSIDER THIS

Could the high place of glory in your heart and mine become the low place of humble service that it was for Jesus?

It is a common notion that we see the world not *as it is*, but *as we are*. In other words, none of us sees the world objectively; we have perspectives and sight based on our brains and heart, and we look for certain things in order to see them.

What the devil saw as a high place for Jesus, and what celebrities and politicians see as a high place for themselves, was a *low place* for Jesus. Jesus was seeing the high place not as it was, but as *he* was.

For Jesus, the high place in his heart had just taken place in his baptism. He was seen by his Father, and he saw his Father and the Spirit at the same time. Jesus's experience of love in those waters, I will contend, was the high point of his life. To know we are seen by God, to have our identity and purpose spoken clearly by God, to be overwhelmed by God's great affection for us—that is the high place in Jesus's heart.

But the best the devil had to offer was from a vantage point for self-serving power, acclaim, and privilege. He wanted to give Jesus the power to do whatever he wanted, with whomever he wanted, wherever he wanted.

He was chipping away at Jesus's wants—his desires—and was finding Jesus's desires utterly foreign to the ones that haunted other human beings.

Could the highest place in your heart and mine become the low place of humble service that it was for Jesus—a low place of humble fellowship with God, humble communion with others on the same journey into Christ, humble worship oriented around seeing the world served, the poor fed, the captives set free, and the human heart loved back to life?

Glancing ahead, in Luke 4, Jesus will leave the wild in the power of the Spirit, enter a synagogue, and begin to proclaim the high places of the kingdom of God—places where "the year of the Lord's favor" (v. 19) does not mean acclaim or big houses, but rather the transformation of the human heart by Christians offering selfless, cruciform love in Jesus's name.

The devil's high place was a low place to Jesus; Jesus's high place was a low place to the devil. He couldn't be convinced of what many hearts today are so easily convinced of—that power turned upon oneself, the accumulation of wealth, the honor offered by others, even the acclaim that comes from generosity and benevolence—is the highest place that one could attain.

Jesus blessed what was unseen. And he knew that changing a human heart was worth more than all the kingdoms of the world.

We can live from this perspective, that to "act justly and to love mercy and to walk humbly" (Micah 6:8) with our God is the highest place to which we could be led.

The devil simply took Jesus to the wrong place. He wasn't tempted, because his heart wasn't in it. In this, Jesus passed the test that Israel's kings and power brokers, even the great King David, never could.

THE PRAYER

Lord of the Wild, our high place is fed by the vision of the good life, the high place, that is pumped our way by media of every sort. We choose to feed our vision of the good life, the high place, by choosing the low place and humbly serving in loving communion with you. In Jesus's name, amen.

THE QUESTIONS

- How does the low place of service feel in comparison to the devil's high place of honor and accumulation? What are the differences in the feelings associated with each, and how can we train our hearts to love the feeling that comes with the former?

AND SHOWED HIM IN AN INSTANT

LUKE 4:1–5

Jesus, full of the Holy Spirit, left the Jordan and was led by the Spirit into the wilderness, where for forty days he was tempted by the devil. He ate nothing during those days, and at the end of them he was hungry.

The devil said to him, "If you are the Son of God, tell this stone to become bread."

Jesus answered, "It is written: 'Man shall not live on bread alone.'"

The devil led him up to a high place *and showed him in an instant* all the kingdoms of the world.

CONSIDER THIS

What we see in an instant, at a glance and while our dopamine is triggered, can disorder our desires.

In an instant, everything can change.

Why does this passage include the phrase "in an instant" before "all the kingdoms of the world"? Other translations say, "in a moment of time." Speed seems to be part of the meaning here.

Why does that matter in this second temptation?

In his book, *The Ruthless Elimination of Hurry: How to Stay Emotionally Healthy and Spiritually Alive in the Chaos of the Modern World*, John Mark Comer writes: "Because what you give your attention to is the person you become. Put another way: the mind is the portal to the soul, and what you fill your mind with will shape the trajectory of your character. In the end, your life is no more than the sum of what you gave your attention to."[14] In other words, be careful little eyes what you see.

Attention. Focus. Speed. The average person touches their smartphone 2,600 or more times per day (low estimate). This distracting habit is linked to decreased productivity, poorer relationships (inattention/presence), memory loss, and habit-formation and addiction based on the constant dopamine hit. Social media, again, a quick read on the world and the opinions of all our "friends," is a psychological environment as our focus becomes our reality.

We are not all-powerful robots, filtering out the bad and only taking in the good. We see it, and we absorb it. We must train our young ones to avert their eyes from what will snake around them later and drag their spirits down. That's not intense parenting. That is preemptive self-help 101.

Hurry and immediate desire gratification are hurricanes, spinning out of control, and are sweeping up many across the globe with their force. We have become people who want things in an instant, without delay—delivered to us almost as soon as we desire them.

Jesus did not live in our fast world as a human being pre-resurrection. He lived in a slow world, where seeing "all the kingdoms" would be a longer-than-lifetime process of viewing drawings and paintings, listening to oral descriptions by travelers, or reading narratives about other lands and using one's imagination.

---

14. Comer, *The Ruthless Elimination of Hurry*, 54–55.

The devil showed Jesus all of it in an instant. It was an "Internet Google images search" before it existed.

What we let in through our eye gate matters for the persuasion of our emotions. We must guard what we see in an instant. Our phones have our attention, and what has our attention is what we become and, inevitably, what we begin to value.

Jesus saw it all in an instant, and speed is one of the enemy's tools of persuasion. Slow down, un-hurry your life, remove yourself for seasons from the instantaneous gratification of your phone—and practice examining the choices before you in light of your identity in Christ and your God-ordained vocation in the world.

THE PRAYER

Lord of the Wild, we are addicted to the instant-and-in-the-moment in our day. We surrender our need for constant visual and mental stimulation through our phones, through social media, through on-demand video, and through constant texting. We want to ruthlessly eliminate hurry so we can move slowly and deliberately—resisting the enemy's speed scheme to deform our faith. In Jesus's name, amen.

THE QUESTION

- What could you do today, even immediately, to slow down your pace of inner and outer life?

23

ALL THE KINGDOMS
OF THE WORLD

LUKE 4:1–5

Jesus, full of the Holy Spirit, left the Jordan and was led by the Spirit into
the wilderness, where for forty days he was tempted by the devil. He
ate nothing during those days, and at the end of them he was hungry.

The devil said to him, "If you are the Son of God,
tell this stone to become bread."

Jesus answered, "It is written: 'Man shall not live on bread alone.'"

The devil led him up to a high place and showed him
in an instant *all the kingdoms of the world*.

CONSIDER THIS

All gain, no pain. That is often the enemy's play. Watch for it and
resist the temptation to believe it is possible.

No eternal gain comes without some sacrifice, some pain, in the
present. We must lose our life in order to find it (Matt. 16:25).

With the click of a button, Jesus is taken to a high place (which is
a horribly low place to him, compared to his high place, which is a
holy low place!) and is shown, instantly *all the kingdoms of the world*.

Impressive. A kingdom is a sphere of influence, a non-locational space where someone exerts their rule and reign over people, land, and more. (Note: the greatest kings, queens, presidents, and politicians of history have never been able to exert lordship over the weather—a visual sign of God's inexorable kingdom ruling overall.)

The devil, the satan, using the only tools in his arsenal to un-name, un-seat, and dis-order Jesus's desires pulls out a big one—all the impressive arenas of control exerted in the world.

I like to see kingdoms, in this case, metaphorically rather than as geopolitical cities, states, countries, and alliances. For example, the kingdom of education. The kingdom of entertainment. The kingdom of finance and economy. The kingdom of science and technology. The kingdom of government and leadership. The kingdom of animals and creation. The kingdom of home and family. The kingdom of the human heart. The kingdom of inner and outer space. We could go on.

As these are revealed to Jesus, in an instant, Jesus hears the future whisper of this song, this word, spoken in a time to come. It may have been spoken into his heart at his baptism, but who knows: "The seventh angel sounded his trumpet, and there were loud voices in heaven, which said: 'The kingdom of the world has become the kingdom of our Lord and of his Messiah, and he will reign for ever and ever'" (Rev. 11:15).

Imagine the devil saying, "Jesus, you can have now what you'll have to wait to get through deep suffering (the "in an instant" temptation is leveraged again). This cup could pass from you." (The enemy may have been with him in the garden later; again, we can't know in what way, but the tone of the garden of Gethsemane text feels similar to the tone of the wild text—only with greater intensity of spiritual labor evidenced on Jesus's part.)

Jesus will receive the kingdoms of this world; the un-namer's play is to offer it all sooner, instantaneously, and without suffering.

All gain, no pain. Now there's a temptation.

That is often the enemy's play. We may have opportunities to get great things through shortcuts, and the enemy will convince us our time has come, our ship has come in, and our big break has arrived.

But the Holy Spirit within us will whisper: "There is a greater kingdom coming your way than this; don't fall for short-term gain and long-term loss—choose the better way of long-term gain and short-term loss. It is the way of the cross."

THE PRAYER

Lord of the Wild, we don't usually want entire kingdoms to be under our rule and reign—but we do want great gain with little cost. Spirit of God, our calling in Christ, the sound of our name being spoken by you and an invitation to partner with you in a great healing in someone's life, is of greater value to us than our comfort. Help our hearts to own this, to become convinced, that the eternal gain being achieved is more beautiful than the short-term glories with which we are tempted. In Jesus's name, amen.

THE QUESTION

- Most of us are pain resistant, in some way, shape, or form. Is there pain in your life right now that you know is yielding in you a greater glory—a greater Christlikeness—than you could achieve without it?

DAN WILT

24

AND HE SAID TO HIM

LUKE 4:1–6

Jesus, full of the Holy Spirit, left the Jordan and was led by the Spirit into the wilderness, where for forty days he was tempted by the devil. He ate nothing during those days, and at the end of them he was hungry.

The devil said to him, "If you are the Son of God, tell this stone to become bread."

Jesus answered, "It is written: 'Man shall not live on bread alone.'"

The devil led him up to a high place and showed him in an instant all the kingdoms of the world. *And he said to him*, "I will give you all their authority and splendor; it has been given to me, and I can give it to anyone I want to."

CONSIDER THIS

Let's revisit how the enemy speaks to us. Earlier in our meditation, we noted that the images of the devil we have from the first thousand or so years of art history, including the images we get from Dante, Milton, and others, are not *biblical*.

Though Jesus may have seen the devil in a way we can't, as a physicalized evil, biblically the satan is understood to be the influence of evil, the personal presence of evil, inviting us to sin and break covenant with God—or to ultimately extinguish our own life and/or the lives of others. We see the evil one at work explicitly in a mass shooting or a suicide.

But more often the enemy is at work, insidiously, speaking into our hearts and minds ideas and thoughts that disorder our desires from the desires of Christ.

When the devil spoke to Jesus, we don't know how that conversation took place. But I believe, even with our limited spiritual sight, the battle of words had similar qualities to ours. We are going our way in life, then a dark thought catches ahold of our minds and we catastrophize about it for weeks on end.

Life is being stolen. That is what the word of the enemy does. Like the devourer himself, the extinguisher of inward and outward life (see Madeleine L'Engle's book in her fiction series, *A Wind in the Door*), the word of satan comes to steal, kill, and destroy (John 10:10).

To hear the voice of God is to be given to. To hear the voice of the enemy is to be taken from. To hear the voice of God is to be brought to life. To hear the voice of the enemy is to be drawn to death.

If you hear hope in the inner thoughts you are entertaining, feed them with the promises of the Word of God (and your favorite songs of worship). If you hear despair in the inner thoughts you are entertaining, confront them with the Word of God and reorient with your favorite songs of worship and the blessed words and prayers of the faithful.

The devil will speak to you, just as the devil spoke to Jesus. The devil will seek to cause you to lose faith in your name before God—Beloved—and your calling in God to live out your covenant life as a son or daughter of your loving heavenly Father before others, inviting them to come alive to do the same.

Here's to hearing God and responding with joy. And here's to hearing the devil (because you will) and responding with the Word of God, the sword of the Spirit, and the promises and the praises of Jesus.

THE PRAYER

Lord of the Wild, it is not our desire to hear the devil speak to us, but it is an inevitability in this fallen world. Train us, by your Spirit within and through habits that we choose to cultivate in faith, to resist that voice with an arsenal of your Word we have pre-hidden in our hearts. In Jesus's name, amen.

THE QUESTIONS

- Are you learning to distinguish the voice of God from your own voice, or the voice of the enemy? If so, what are you learning?

I WILL GIVE YOU ALL THEIR AUTHORITY AND SPLENDOR

LUKE 4:1–6

Jesus, full of the Holy Spirit, left the Jordan and was led by the Spirit into the wilderness, where for forty days he was tempted by the devil. He ate nothing during those days, and at the end of them he was hungry.

The devil said to him, "If you are the Son of God, tell this stone to become bread."

Jesus answered, "It is written: 'Man shall not live on bread alone.'"

The devil led him up to a high place and showed him in an instant all the kingdoms of the world. And he said to him, *"I will give you all their authority and splendor;* it has been given to me, and I can give it to anyone I want to."

CONSIDER THIS

Ever wish you had control—of people and situations and outcomes? Ever wish you had resources—of money and influence and power? Or have you ever had a position of influence, and you controlled people and situations with it? Or have you ever had a platform, and you fed on praise from others to meet a hole within your heart?

Each time we add a new word or phrase from the passage, we are leaving the previous parts of the passage there. Why? The Hebrew word for meditation ("who meditates on his law day and night," Ps. 1:2) is the word *hagah* and carries in it the idea that it is by mulling over, repeating continually, chewing on (like a dog with a bone), and lingering in passages in the Word of God that the riches of the meditation literature that is the Scriptures can be fully savored and their flavor extracted.

That is what we are doing with this passage, and the Holy Spirit will continue to give us insights as we read it over and over, now with new light shining on it given during the time and space we have set aside for taking in the mysteries of God's Word.

Today, the words of the devil to Jesus, in the second temptation, weigh heavy on us—because we see our desires laid bare in them.

"I will give you all their authority and splendor."

Authority, when the devil is talking about it, means something different than when God is talking about it. The satanic version of authority is authoritarian—it means sole oversight; control; the power to do what you want, when you want, any way you want; arrogant and self-serving leadership; and a lack of accountability.

Splendor, when the devil is talking about it, means something different than when God is talking about it. The satanic version of splendor is self-focused remarkability and self-glory. It means attractive, desirous, above the less beautiful, shiny, and impressive.

The devil is seeking to unseat and unsettle Jesus from his core vocation as the humble and self-giving Son of God who will take on the character of the Suffering Servant from Isaiah 53: "He had no beauty or majesty to attract us to him, nothing in his appearance that we should desire him. He was despised and rejected by mankind, a man of suffering, and familiar with pain. Like one from whom people hide their faces he was despised, and we held him in low esteem" (vv. 2b–3).

Jesus's vision of the worldly authority of earthly kingdoms contrasted with his view of holy kingship; he didn't need human authority to get his work of loving, serving, dying, and rising done. He did not need, nor want, a president's title, a prime minister's power, nor a prince's purview.

Jesus's vision of the worldly splendor of earthly kingdoms contrasted with his view of the kingdom of God; he didn't need remarkable cities, opulent palaces, or exciting entertainment to get his work done of loving, serving, dying, and raising up a movement of covenant people operating within his unseen rule and reign.

The same temptations come to us. Would you like absolute control, so no one can hurt you, and people will simply do what you want without pushing back? Would you like wealth and beauty, and all that the kingdoms of this world have to offer without needing to follow God or have any parameters on your freedom?

Jesus rejects the enemy's vision of authority and splendor, and the attraction of the kingdoms of this world. We stand with Jesus, in seeing and promoting a kingdom that is not of this world—and subverts the values of these earthly kingdoms in every aspect. Humbly, we walk forward, in the authority and splendor only a child of God can be robed in.

Lord of the Wild, this temptation tugs on our hearts as those who live in this world, often with struggle and heartache, following you in a foreign territory. Fill our inward imaginations with a vision of a kingdom that endures forever and, ultimately, heals the human heart—including our own. In Jesus's name, amen.

THE QUESTIONS

- What areas of control and splendor have most tempted you in the world's kingdoms? How and where have you found strength to overcome their draw?

26

IT HAS BEEN GIVEN TO ME, AND I CAN GIVE IT

LUKE 4:1–6

Jesus, full of the Holy Spirit, left the Jordan and was led by the Spirit into the wilderness, where for forty days he was tempted by the devil. He ate nothing during those days, and at the end of them he was hungry.

The devil said to him, "If you are the Son of God, tell this stone to become bread."

Jesus answered, "It is written: 'Man shall not live on bread alone.'"

The devil led him up to a high place and showed him in an instant all the kingdoms of the world. And he said to him, "I will give you all their authority and splendor; *it has been given to me, and I can give it* to anyone I want to."

CONSIDER THIS

The enemy has power, and according to Ephesians 2:2, that power and its tentacle powers permeate the air we breathe and the world in which we live. We should not take that lightly. We're in a battle, and if we forget that truth, we will be taken out.

Just as a genie in a bottle can grant three wishes, the enemy has some Trojan-horse prizes to deliver to the soul that surrenders to its desires. Those prizes always look good on the outside; the satan's offerings don't look evil, smell evil, or convey evil—at least not immediately. They are like poison hidden in candy; the devil's promises are veiled in innocence and possibility. They seem healing and satisfying—then they sting with the strike of a scorpion.

The small pleasures the enemy offers can become heart desires—desires radically out of alignment with those Christ is forming in us. We think we are on the way of life, and we find out what we did, what we chose, how we acted, has us firmly on the way of death and pain. Just as two lines that run close together but slowly diverge, we move with confidence until some shock, some trouble precipitated by our slowly growing sin wakes us up to just how far we are from home. We give an inch, and the devil takes a mile.

This is where Jesus's vocation, being clear and settled in his affections and disposition, held him. The enemy had the power to give him all the splendor and authority of the kingdoms of the world. Jesus knew he could, and perhaps the Son of Man could have been tempted more strongly if the enemy threw in the kingdom of heaven. But the devil has no authority over the kingdom of heaven—it looks nothing like what his rule over the kingdoms of this world looks like.

Let's read all of Ephesians 2:1–7 to orient to how Jesus calls us to face the same temptation from the one who has power to give it all:

> As for you, you were dead in your transgressions and sins, in which you used to live when you followed the ways of this world and of the ruler of the kingdom of the air, the spirit who is now at work in those who are disobedient. All of us also lived among them at one time, gratifying the cravings of our flesh and following its desires and thoughts. Like the rest, we were by nature

deserving of wrath. But because of his great love for us, God, who is rich in mercy, made us alive with Christ even when we were dead in transgressions—it is by grace you have been saved. And God raised us up with Christ and seated us with him in the heavenly realms in Christ Jesus, in order that in the coming ages he might show the incomparable riches of his grace, expressed in his kindness to us in Christ Jesus.

Who needs the kingdoms of this world when we have been seated in heavenly realms with Christ, priests and royalty, mastered by a love that is healing us, daily, from the inside out?

Ephesians 1:18–23 affirms our kingdom riches and Jesus's power to give them:

I pray that the eyes of your heart may be enlightened in order that you may know the hope to which he has called you, the riches of his glorious inheritance in his holy people, and his incomparably great power for us who believe. That power is the same as the mighty strength he exerted when he raised Christ from the dead and seated him at his right hand in the heavenly realms, far above all rule and authority, power and dominion, and every name that is invoked, not only in the present age but also in the one to come. And God placed all things under his feet and appointed him to be head over everything for the church, which is his body, the fullness of him who fills everything in every way.

Ephesians 6:10–12 gives us the way to face down the enemy and his promises of a better life than the Lord would provide: "Finally, be strong in the Lord and in his mighty power. Put on the full armor of God, so that you can take your stand against the devil's schemes. For our struggle is not against flesh and blood, but against the rulers, against the authorities, against the powers of this dark world and against the spiritual forces of evil in the heavenly realms."

Sometimes, our greatest work is just to stand against the enemy's promises. Find the community around you that will fan the truth of God in you into flame, that will help you resist the candy-coated poison the enemy is seeking to feed every single one of us.

THE PRAYER

Lord of the Wild, we are drawn to the things this world gives; some we are drawn to more than others. But in the end, each leads to death. Root up in us any love of money, fame, power, influence, pleasure, or advantage over another that leads to death and disrupts our walk on the path of life. In Jesus's name, amen.

THE QUESTION

- How have you found strength to stand firm in resisting promises the world gives, staying with Jesus on the path to life?

27

TO ANYONE I WANT TO

LUKE 4:1–6

Jesus, full of the Holy Spirit, left the Jordan and was led by the Spirit into the wilderness, where for forty days he was tempted by the devil. He ate nothing during those days, and at the end of them he was hungry.

The devil said to him, "If you are the Son of God, tell this stone to become bread."

Jesus answered, "It is written: 'Man shall not live on bread alone.'"

The devil led him up to a high place and showed him in an instant all the kingdoms of the world. And he said to him, "I will give you all their authority and splendor; it has been given to me, and I can give it *to anyone I want to*."

CONSIDER THIS

What does it feel like to be chosen? We've probably all had experiences where someone had the agency to make a choice about us—to pick us for a team, to pick us for a friend, to pick us for a spouse, or to pick us for a job. Something inside us wants to feel special, to be chosen, to be selected from among the masses.

The Father called Jesus by name. It is clear that Jesus was chosen. The Father picked him, in front of everyone, affirming it in a profound way. But the Father had a long plan for that choosing, a plan Jesus intuitively must have known would involve tremendous and vicarious suffering (Isa. 53), a cup he would prefer to pass (Matt. 26:39), and a torn-down temple (John 2:19). Being chosen to enjoy unspeakable intimacy with the Father—and to suffer—does that feel like being picked for God's best?

So the enemy makes a play based on making Jesus feel chosen—with a more pleasurable and immediate result than what Jesus would inevitably face. "Yes, Father," I would say. "But suffering? Isn't there another way?" The enemy has another way.

"I can give it to anyone I want to."

If Jesus had wavered, even for a moment, as the Son of Man, offered kingdoms and selected as the one chosen by the evil one (who apparently had power to make the offer), you and I would be lost—far from God and without hope (Eph. 2:12).

When you are invited to have a platform, you have been chosen. When you see your gifts being appreciated and effective in a school, in a church, in a business, on a board, or in a group—it is tempting to believe that *we* are the reason we were chosen.

And the enemy begins to whisper, inaudibly, and often sounding like the God he resists: "You are special, you are chosen; this opportunity you have has everything to do with your gifts, your experience, and your obedience. You deserve this. Revel in it."

That's when the call from the Father comes (here, spoken through Paul to the Philippians):

> Therefore if you have any encouragement from being united with Christ, if any comfort from his love, if any common sharing in the Spirit, if any tenderness and compassion, then make my joy complete by being

like-minded, having the same love, being one in spirit and of one mind. Do nothing out of selfish ambition or vain conceit. Rather, in humility value others above yourselves, not looking to your own interests but each of you to the interests of the others.

In your relationships with one another, have the same mindset as Christ Jesus: Who, being in very nature God, did not consider equality with God something to be used to his own advantage; rather, he made himself nothing by taking the very nature of a servant, being made in human likeness. And being found in appearance as a man, he humbled himself by becoming obedient to death—even death on a cross!

Therefore God exalted him to the highest place and gave him the name that is above every name, that at the name of Jesus every knee should bow, in heaven and on earth and under the earth, and every tongue acknowledge that Jesus Christ is Lord, to the glory of God the Father. (Phil. 2:1–11)

The Father has chosen you and named you. No matter the successes you must bear, no matter the suffering you must bear, you have been selected by your heavenly Father with love to come into the fullness of the character of Christ. It will cost you. Do not look back. The enemy will make you easier offers, in the quiet of your heart. Resist them; the end we look toward, brother, sister, is the salvation of our souls:

In all this you greatly rejoice, though now for a little while you may have had to suffer grief in all kinds of trials. These have come so that the proven genuineness of your faith—of greater worth than gold, which perishes even though refined by fire—may result in praise, glory and honor when Jesus Christ is revealed. Though you have not seen him, you love him; and even though you do not see him now, you believe in him and are filled with an inexpressible and glorious joy, for you are receiving the end result of your faith, the salvation of your souls. (1 Peter 1:6–9)

I am moved to pray a prayer like this after reading these words of life: I am chosen (1 Peter 2:9) along with followers of your way. It is enough for me to serve alongside you to the point of life or to the point of death.

THE PRAYER

Lord of the Wild, we have been chosen to be a precious child of the Father, a chosen ambassador of your presence (1 Peter 2:9) in the world. We choose to rest in this choosing, no matter what flattery may come our way. We resist the pull of believing the lie that our own specialness has made a way for us. We choose to serve, and to walk away from self-sufficiency. In Jesus's name, amen.

THE QUESTIONS

- Are there any areas of influence or ministry you have been given that you feel entitled to or entitled from the fruits of your work? How could you return to the servant-hearted, open-handed leadership posture of Jesus as you move forward?

IF (PART TWO)

LUKE 4:1–7

Jesus, full of the Holy Spirit, left the Jordan and was led by the Spirit into the wilderness, where for forty days he was tempted by the devil. He ate nothing during those days, and at the end of them he was hungry.

The devil said to him, "If you are the Son of God, tell this stone to become bread."

Jesus answered, "It is written: 'Man shall not live on bread alone.'"

The devil led him up to a high place and showed him in an instant all the kingdoms of the world. And he said to him, "I will give you all their authority and splendor; it has been given to me, and I can give it to anyone I want to. *If* you worship me, it will all be yours."

CONSIDER THIS

If.

There it is again. For the second time in the testing, the temptation, of Jesus in the wild, this simple two-letter word appears again.

I'm incredibly confident in who I am in Christ—until a dark voice in my mind questions me: "Why are you so confident in who you are in Christ? Have you met you lately? You're fearful, anxious, proud, forgetful, and you lack both trust and compassion. You should question if you are enough; if you'll even make it through this life and finish halfway well. You're not such a healthy person, let alone a disciple of Jesus."

If.

Jesus has already had his Sonship and his captive-releasing vocation (all embodied in his Sonship, the purest essence of his calling) questioned, right after its declaration in his baptism by John in the Jordan. He's pulled through, and modeled the way through for you and me, having been "tempted . . . as we are—yet he did not sin" (Heb. 4:15).

But this second if is different from the first. This if represents a key, a doorway, to a better destiny.

This is the kind of if filling the pages of books, the Internet, and the social media promises of self-made entrepreneurs around the world. *If you do this, that, and the other thing, you will get this result.* That is not to say that some of the ifs out there don't work; they do. But in working in their limited way, they can displace the better way that leads to a different kind of good life than they promise.

The quality of the promise must match the quality of the result; better confidence, better skin, better attitudes, better memory, better muscle tone, better relationships, and better political results all fall short of the result of a heart, home, church, city, and world made new.

So, while a president or prime minister promises a bright, bold future for the greatest nation on the earth if they are elected, the promise can never match reality. The world will be remade, and the kingdoms of this world will become the kingdoms of our Lord and of his Christ, and he will reign forever (Rev. 11:15). The golden age will come when the one true King ushers it in; not when a politician has control of a tiny kingdom's administrative reigns for four years of all human history.

"If you worship me," is the key offered to the door of a suffering-less path for Jesus. All gain, no groan. All power, no pain.

It's tempting; I would be lying if I said it wasn't. If I simply stop worshipping God—which is the equivalent of worshipping the satan—I might be able to have a life with limited suffering. I like the sound of a life with limited or no suffering.

But you know the sound I look forward to more? I look forward to the sound of my Father welcoming me into eternity with the words, "Well done, good and faithful servant. . . . Come and share your master's happiness!" (Matt. 25:21).

That's the sound we all want to hear.

THE PRAYER

Lord of the Wild, we're not above disconnecting our worship from you, and turning all that praise and confidence toward ourselves. In so doing, we would worship, ultimately, the enemy who seeks to destroy and de-story us. We choose to stay in your story, to worship you only. In Jesus's name, amen.

THE QUESTIONS

- Have you ever followed the "if you do this, then this will happen" strategies to the good life offered in this world? What was your experience, and did it ultimately help you grow in your faith?

DAN WILT

YOU WORSHIP ME

LUKE 4:1–7

Jesus, full of the Holy Spirit, left the Jordan and was led by the Spirit into the wilderness, where for forty days he was tempted by the devil. He ate nothing during those days, and at the end of them he was hungry.

The devil said to him, "If you are the Son of God, tell this stone to become bread."

Jesus answered, "It is written: 'Man shall not live on bread alone.'"

The devil led him up to a high place and showed him in an instant all the kingdoms of the world. And he said to him, "I will give you all their authority and splendor; it has been given to me, and I can give it to anyone I want to. If *you worship me*, it will all be yours."

CONSIDER THIS

Let's continue with the idea that to cease worshipping God is to begin worshipping the enemy of our souls. You've heard before, most probably, that the word *worship* comes from the Old English word meaning "worth-ship." We worship what we value most. And what we value most becomes the ordering principle of our lives.

"Watch what you value," becomes the operating principle for a life staying on a trajectory into Christ.

While it is helpful to understand evil in terms of a personified spirit, like the satan, the devil, and the accuser, it is also helpful to understand evil in terms of the pervasive influence of the self in society.

When I make myself and my pleasure my highest value, my highest vision of the good life, then I am worshipping the devil. Pause here. How many Christians do you know who put the lion's share of their energies into saving, investing, and bettering the lives of themselves and their families, while giving less-than-sacrificial support to the poor, the dying, the martyred, the disillusioned, the fearful, and the marginalized all around them?

I don't want to say as Christians that we can think we're worshipping God while having an actual value-set that shows a different priority base—but I must. I must because this may be me, at least in times of stress and trouble. I turn toward self-preservation, self-protection—and if something gets in my way, even a sacrificial need, I am quick to say yes to me and mine and ours.

Please hear me: we should be wise and steward our resources toward self-care and family care. I'm not saying we shouldn't. I'm saying that idols arise easily in this life and are masters at subtle entry into our value system. We must be alert to the diversion of our worship, of the inner assignment of highest value, to such things.

As my brother-in-law, a New Testament scholar, often reminds me: Idolatry leads to injustice; when I forget who I am, I forget who you are—and I make you a means to my ends. Dehumanization and tribalism follow; we move toward self-preservation and place life-offering servanthood to the side while we fight our tribalistic battles to win the war.

I'm convinced the worship of the devil is not so obvious; it is evidenced in a heart that has made its outward priorities an inward map of their motivations, motivations clearly pointed back at one's own care above others. I'm a big fan of self-care. But it's not the goal; rather, it is a means to wholeness and fruitfulness for the sake of renewing our call to sonship and daughterhood in the world.

As Paul writes to the Philippians in 2:3–4, 21: "Do nothing out of selfish ambition or vain conceit. Rather, in humility value others above yourselves, not looking to your own interests but each of you to the interests of the others. . . . For everyone looks out for their own interests, not those of Jesus Christ."

Lord, let us be those who look out for the interests of others—worshipping you above ourselves and the world of pleasure options around us.

THE PRAYER

Lord of the Wild, our story is interwoven with yours, and we desire to worship the Father in spirit and in truth (John 4:24) with no reserves held back for our own vision of the good life. Come, Lord, find in us hearts that value you and your Word above all things. In Jesus's name, amen.

THE QUESTION

- How has the worship of self, or your own vision of the good life, subtly displaced your worship of God over the years?

3 0

IT WILL ALL BE YOURS

Jesus, full of the Holy Spirit, left the Jordan and was led by the Spirit into
the wilderness, where for forty days he was tempted by the devil. He
ate nothing during those days, and at the end of them he was hungry.

The devil said to him, "If you are the Son of God,
tell this stone to become bread."

Jesus answered, "It is written: 'Man shall not live on bread alone.'"

The devil led him up to a high place and showed him in an instant
all the kingdoms of the world. And he said to him, "I will give you all
their authority and splendor; it has been given to me, and I can give
it to anyone I want to. If you worship me, *it will all be yours*."

CONSIDER THIS

The second temptation of Jesus in the wild ends with a punch line.

That punch line is *ownership*.

"It will all be yours."

I imagine that Jesus heard a verse in his mind, from Israel's prayer
book, the book of Psalms, at that very moment. "The earth is the
LORD's," said the writer of Psalm 24:1, "and everything in it, the
world, and all who live in it."

You've probably heard the idea that we are not owners in this life; rather, we are stewards of what God has entrusted to us. Like me, you've probably entertained it for many years, especially if you were taught about money from a biblical perspective. And many of us, including me, have agreed and aspired to this idea to one degree or another.

But Jesus didn't have the latitude of degrees as an option, as we often think we do. Jesus knew that it was not all his, nor was it all his to own. He saw the world belonging to his Father and to imagine it belonging to himself, rather than to his Father, was repulsive.

What if we began, as followers of the way of Jesus, to resist language that proclaimed ultimate ownership—of our cars, our homes, our money, our work, or even our families—and chose the language of stewardship in its place? How would our minds and perspectives change slowly over time? How would we treat the resources now flowing through our hands, rather than finding their resting place in us?

When we face a financial difficulty, or a difficulty with something we perceive is in our possession (like a house or car), my wife leads us in the spirit of Psalm 24:1. She says something like, "Lord, your house needs a new roof. We look forward to how you will provide for that." Every time she says something like that, I am reoriented from the trouble and made aware that the Father has a way, whether I perceive it or not.

The Milky Way, the stars, the skies, the mountains, the fields, and the relationships all around us belong to the Lord. For that reason, they are gifts given to us to share joy in, to freely distribute to others, and to delight in and pass on that delight to others.

It is good to know the Lord takes care of what he owns, that we don't have to worry and fear. What the Father owns he provides for and shares with us. We don't need to own the things the Father already does.

We don't need it to all be ours. In fact, it's better if it's not, because often what comes, goes; what lives, dies; what starts, finishes. In those moments we can be thankful for what runs through our hands and hearts, but ultimately goes back to the Father.

THE PRAYER

Lord of the Wild, we choose to begin to use the language of stewardship going forward, acknowledging that you own all things and have our deepest concerns in mind. In Jesus's name, amen.

THE QUESTION

- How have you used the language of ownership in your own life, and how would shifting to the language of stewardship change your perspective on sharing what you have?

JESUS ANSWERED (PART TWO)

LUKE 4:1–8

Jesus, full of the Holy Spirit, left the Jordan and was led by the Spirit into the wilderness, where for forty days he was tempted by the devil. He ate nothing during those days, and at the end of them he was hungry.

The devil said to him, "If you are the Son of God, tell this stone to become bread."

Jesus answered, "It is written: 'Man shall not live on bread alone.'"

The devil led him up to a high place and showed him in an instant all the kingdoms of the world. And he said to him, "I will give you all their authority and splendor; it has been given to me, and I can give it to anyone I want to. If you worship me, it will all be yours."

Jesus answered, "It is written: 'Worship the Lord your God and serve him only.'"

CONSIDER THIS

Jesus is not going to leave anything undone in the wild. He chooses to have an answer for every offer made to him to leave his name behind and to choose a lesser vocation. He answers—and the work of the Christian is the same.

When the world declares its answers to the racial issues of our time, we answer—with the Word of God and the call to see others as our brothers and sisters and family.

When the world declares its answers to the political issues of our time, we answer—we declare our allegiance to the one true God and defy any political party that makes him a mascot of their ideology.

When the world declares its answers to the sexual issues of our time, we answer—we declare that our bodies and our identity belong to the Lord, and that no narration of a disordered creation will displace his promises to love us and heal us with his restoring affection.

Christians do not have all the answers and, sometimes, we must be silent as the world presses in on us, demanding we say something. Often those taunts come from a polarizing motive, a desire to claim us as part of their percentage or dismiss us as enemies.

But answers we must have, and the Word of God is where we begin. Yes, the Word is nuanced, and must be understood deeply and well, and in light of the whole counsel of the Scriptures. But we are not left to ourselves and the zeitgeist (the "spirit of the age") of our times. We don't live in an uncared-for creation, in a loveless, cold, and random universe.

We are beloved, and that is the "answer" Jesus received at his baptism. All his other answers, in the wild and throughout the Gospel stories, were derivatives of this answer: "For God so loved the world, that he gave" (John 3:16). Our God is a giver, and we don't need the enemy's distributions to store up for ourselves treasures in this life: "Do not store up for yourselves treasures on earth, where moths and vermin destroy, and where thieves break in and steal. But store up for yourselves treasures in heaven, where moths and vermin do not destroy, and where thieves do not break in and steal" (Matt. 6:19–20).

We are in love-training, and Jesus, our Master, has preceded us in loving that which the Father loves, gives, and provides for us in this life.

We must answer the spirit of our age, when it creeps into our mind to convince us we own more, need more, want more, and should get more than the Father is giving. We can't paint a pretty face on greed and call it holy ambition; nor can we fill a baptismal and baptize our consumerism to make it holy.

To want what the Father wants for us; this is what Jesus did, and what the wild will teach us to do if we let it. When the going gets tough, answer the enemy you face. It will shut him down for the next round and leave no room for your heart to wander.

THE PRAYER

Lord of the Wild, we have often lacked an answer for the enemy's temptation, and it creates room for us to let him have his way. Teach us to answer—with your Word, your promises, and your vision of the life you intend for a child of God. In Jesus's name, amen.

THE QUESTIONS

- What could you begin to practice now in order to better answer the enemy's temptations later? Are you doing it, or are you planning to start?

IT IS WRITTEN (PART TWO)

LUKE 4:1–8

Jesus, full of the Holy Spirit, left the Jordan and was led by the Spirit into the wilderness, where for forty days he was tempted by the devil. He ate nothing during those days, and at the end of them he was hungry.

The devil said to him, "If you are the Son of God, tell this stone to become bread."

Jesus answered, "It is written: 'Man shall not live on bread alone.'"

The devil led him up to a high place and showed him in an instant all the kingdoms of the world. And he said to him, "I will give you all their authority and splendor; it has been given to me, and I can give it to anyone I want to. If you worship me, it will all be yours."

Jesus answered, "*It is written*: 'Worship the Lord your God and serve him only.'"

CONSIDER THIS

I love the Word of God.

Recently, with a friend, I wrote two books of prayers based on all 150 Psalms. We lingered for more than three years in that work, constantly feasting on, meditating in, considering, weighing, and praying the Word of God. I was changed through the holy labor of love, and I'm still ringing—as Annie Dillard put it in her book, *Pilgrim at Tinker Creek*—like a bell.

I have faced, at various points on my own journey, challenges related to anxiety and depression. The Word of God stabilized me and, energized by the Spirit, kept me from checking out and checking in to an institution. I know that you may resonate with the same sentiment: the Word of God is a Word of Truth, not only in a world of lies, but also when a mind is losing perspective.

The Word of God, given power to work in us by the Spirit of God, enables us to face down the demonic schemes assigned to us by quickening the spirit to embrace God's life rather than relying on our own strength.

We read, sing, or pray the Word of God, and our spirits rise to what is true, what is right, what is pure, what is lovely—and we think on those things (Phil. 4:8).

We may never understand all that the Holy Spirit does. What we can know is this: we can trust in, delight in, enjoy and savor, the written Word of God. It has been a bridge to communion with Jesus, the Living Word of God, time and time and time again. It will continue to be for the rest of our lives.

There is no hell you or I face that cannot be answered by a promise from the Word of God.

THE PRAYER

Lord of the Wild, you answered the enemy with truth—having a command of the Scriptures that you learned through growing up as one of us. Teach us to rehearse your

promises daily, and to delight in memorizing your precepts,
hiding them in our hearts. In Jesus's name, amen.

THE QUESTIONS

- What promise or passage from the Word of God has most strengthened you in your seasons of battle? What is it about that passage that moves you?

33

WORSHIP THE LORD YOUR GOD AND SERVE HIM ONLY

LUKE 4:1–8

Jesus, full of the Holy Spirit, left the Jordan and was led by the Spirit into the wilderness, where for forty days he was tempted by the devil. He ate nothing during those days, and at the end of them he was hungry.

The devil said to him, "If you are the Son of God, tell this stone to become bread."

Jesus answered, "It is written: 'Man shall not live on bread alone.'"

The devil led him up to a high place and showed him in an instant all the kingdoms of the world. And he said to him, "I will give you all their authority and splendor; it has been given to me, and I can give it to anyone I want to. If you worship me, it will all be yours."

Jesus answered, "It is written: '**Worship the Lord your God and serve him only**.'"

CONSIDER THIS

For more than half of my life, since I became a follower of Jesus, I have been drawn to the grand, cosmic, yet very earthy idea of *worship*. I've written and spoken countless words about the topic in books, articles, seminars, and conferences. Over the years I've often asked myself: *Why? Why does this matter so much to you, Dan?*

This passage, where Jesus answers the test, the temptation, of having all this world has to offer without any suffering, is my answer. It draws its strength from Exodus 20:3, the first of the Ten Commandments maintaining covenant between God and his people: "You shall have no other gods before me," and Deuteronomy 6:13a: "Fear the LORD your God, serve him only."

"Worship the Lord your God and serve him only" (Luke 4:8)—it is the only way to find your complete purpose as a human being, and it is the only way to become whole, to heal, in the wearing, tearing storms of life.

A favorite writer on worship, Evelyn Underhill, wrote in 1936: "Worship, in all its grades and kinds, is a response of the creature to the Eternal."[15] Maybe like you, I have come to believe that all we do in worship is a response to our Creator's all-pursuing love. Whether that is a beautiful response, a fitting response, or an all-encompassing response is up to us as individuals and communities.

But worship *is* our response.

What Jesus is doing in this passage is reorienting the devil to the way the world works according to God's driving plan. We worship God, giving him our ultimate love, allegiance, and obedience, serving from a heart given over to a living-sacrifice way of moving through the world, and the worlds of our hearts, homes, churches, and cities.

---

15. Evelyn Underhill, *Worship* (Cambridge: James Clarke & Co., 1936, 1937, 2010), 3.

Our inward and outward failures to worship in spirit and in truth (John 4:20–24) from a pure heart, from a pure life—both personal and communal—bring the crumbling, the crushing, of the soul.

Most of us are drawn to musical expressions of worship. Some of us have had the precious experience of being in environments where there is a high expectation of meeting with God in an intimate way in the worship space. When that worship expectation is well-led by a seasoned, humble, servant-hearted, expectant, rehearsed, and capable musician, and the music is tended as a space for prayer and adoration, amazing things can happen.

I've seen lives turned around completely in a time of worship—a drug dealer weeping as the Spirit of God overwhelms him with love and kindness; a broken marriage experiencing the balm of grace and a renewed capacity to move forward; a young woman who was suicidal walking out full of joy and surrounded by supportive community.

While music is only one way worship happens, it can be powerful in our lives, whether experienced together in community or as we worship in our car with the music blasting and our hearts poured out to God in praise.

Really, adversary? Worship you to gain trinkets and powers that disappear and sicken the soul as they do, or worship God and serve him only? You thought the Son of Man would fall for that? I know that we do, but Jesus led the way in reminding us that worship of God is the way the servant followers of Christ live in this world.

THE PRAYER

Lord of the Wild, it's an astounding thing how you can meet us in worship, in all its forms, reclaiming our hearts and changing our perspective to one of trust and clarity. Thank you. Keep us in the way of worship and show us the ways that will help us resist the enemy's work to un-name us before you in our own lives. In Jesus's name, amen.

THE QUESTIONS

- What does this passage on worship mean to you? How do you worship the Lord your God, and serve him only?

34

THE DEVIL LED HIM TO JERUSALEM

LUKE 4:1–9

Jesus, full of the Holy Spirit, left the Jordan and was led by the Spirit into the wilderness, where for forty days he was tempted by the devil. He ate nothing during those days, and at the end of them he was hungry.

The devil said to him, "If you are the Son of God, tell this stone to become bread."

Jesus answered, "It is written: 'Man shall not live on bread alone.'"

The devil led him up to a high place and showed him in an instant all the kingdoms of the world. And he said to him, "I will give you all their authority and splendor; it has been given to me, and I can give it to anyone I want to. If you worship me, it will all be yours."

Jesus answered, "It is written: 'Worship the Lord your God and serve him only.'"

The devil led him to Jerusalem and had him stand on the highest point of the temple. "If you are the Son of God," he said, "throw yourself down from here."

CONSIDER THIS

We now enter the third test, the third temptation, of Jesus in the wild. His vocation is at stake. He has been named and called by the Father, and the enemy is doing his primary destructive work, knowing all this is at stake. He is seeking to un-name Jesus—to cut off his personhood before the Creator and his ministry of bringing dead things to life before it even begins

In the Madeleine L'Engle science fiction classic, *A Wind in the Door*, she speaks of people who love as "Namers," and the demonic creatures that destroy as "Xers." The Father names us, and our name carries our calling, our purpose, our order in a chaotic world. The adversary un-names us, distorts our identity, and seeks to rip it from us as early as possible in life. That is why it is important to walk with the Lord in our younger years with mature guidance and Christ-oriented support; it is in the early years the enemy sought to strip from us our personhood before God. The Father wants to minister to those places of brokenness; our work is to not sweep them under the rug and hope we somehow outgrew lies we believed early on.

The satan, the accuser, has one shot left. In the first test, he aims at Jesus's use of *power,* pressing him to use it on himself (the bread). In the second test, he aims at Jesus's use of *privilege*, seeking to convince him he can have everything he ever desired without pain or suffering. In this third test, the evil one aims at Jesus's use of *persuasion*—tempting him to perform a miracle that will convince all of his message and enable him to skip the unbelief that will inevitably lead him to a cross.

The devil wants Jesus to put the Lord his God to the test, but the nature of that press is toward a noble end—that all would see his deity.

Why is this such a subtle, important, final play of the enemy? I believe the answer lies in Israel's primary stumbling in their forty years of wilderness wanderings—they asked for things that didn't derive from the Father's will, but rather from their own.

It is willfulness, our own will, that Jesus is being challenged to exert. Jesus will use the gift of his volition to heal the sick, raise the dead, and bring the message of life to millennia of souls like you and me. Could the satan get him to exert his own will to get the Father to do his—rather than the other way around?

A friend and fellow leader once suggested that the difference between prayer and magic is determined by knowing *whose* will is being done. In prayer, true conversation and communion with God, we are interested in seeing the Father's will be done, here on earth as it is in heaven (Matt. 6:9–13). In magic, which prayer can easily and subtly turn into, we use our will and prayer to get God to do *our* will. Whether our will being done is expressed in a chain letter full of "just pass this on to seven people and your prayer will be granted," or is expressed in prayers that rely more on many words (Matt. 6:7) and spiritual badgering of God than trust and obedience, such willfulness and its incantations are about magic— ways to manipulate spiritual power to do what we want.

Jesus will not press his will up against the Father's, persuading God to do something other than what God himself initiates.

THE PRAYER

Lord of the Wild, we have used our own wills to get you to do what we want and ask. That is different than us being honest. That is about prioritizing our will over yours. Forgive us, and give us the will to do your will alone. In Jesus's name, amen.

THE QUESTION

- Have you ever, even for noble reasons, prayed in a way that was more about your will being done than the Father's?

35

AND HAD HIM STAND ON THE HIGHEST POINT OF THE TEMPLE

LUKE 4:1–9

Jesus, full of the Holy Spirit, left the Jordan and was led by the Spirit into the wilderness, where for forty days he was tempted by the devil. He ate nothing during those days, and at the end of them he was hungry.

The devil said to him, "If you are the Son of God, tell this stone to become bread." Jesus answered, "It is written: 'Man shall not live on bread alone.'"

The devil led him up to a high place and showed him in an instant all the kingdoms of the world. And he said to him, "I will give you all their authority and splendor; it has been given to me, and I can give it to anyone I want to. If you worship me, it will all be yours."

Jesus answered, "It is written: 'Worship the Lord your God and serve him only.'"

The devil led him to Jerusalem *and had him stand on the highest point of the temple*. "If you are the Son of God," he said, "throw yourself down from here."

CONSIDER THIS

Have you had platforms in your life—opportunities to speak, teach, guide, lead, or influence in a church, a business, or a project—that you had the humility to use for God's glory and not your own?

I once read an article by a scholar noting that humility was not a valued virtue in a leader, historically and globally, until Jesus came on the scene.

The highest point of the temple, in today's passage, could represent many different tests of the heart—all of them oriented around why high places are different than low places. For one, a high point is more visible than a low place. Leaders lead from on high, from their fortified city, from their elevated throne, from their high popularity and visibility to their people.

With the high supporting one's leadership, or so history has emphasized, we are too normal, too unremarkable, too uninspiring to be influential. But gain a little height with a city, a throne, or a stage of popularity and influence (having a movie credit is not the only way a small-time celebrity gets created)? *Then* you can influence others.

Take the high place, right? Have the influence, in Jesus's name, correct? The answer this story gives us to those questions is no.

No. No. No. No. No.

Jesus tells us to take the lowest place at the table (Luke 14:10), to bow lower than everyone else in the room to wash their feet as a servant (John 13:1–17), to become the least of all if you want to become great (Mark 10:43).

And he did it. Instead of taking the high place of visibility, he chose the long, slow, low work of serving, caring, influencing, and loving his way into the hearts of individuals. He had no impressive form, and as Isaiah 53:3, the passage of the Suffering Servant, prophesied: "He was despised and rejected by mankind, a man of suffering, and familiar with pain. Like one from whom people hide their faces he was despised, and we held him in low esteem."

While Jesus could have taken the high place, displaying God's favor on his life and forcing his will on the Father, he knew that the way of humility and slow, patient grace was the path to changing human hearts.

And one by one, he did it. No big shows, no spiritual fireworks to shut down all questions; just deep, abiding presence, with signs and wonders following. God with us. Immanuel. The man who made himself low to show us the high way of humble love.

THE PRAYER

Lord of the Wild, there is a humility to your way, a deep patience to how you change a heart, that has brought the world to remark about your simple life of love. We choose the low places in which to serve, the unseen places of faithfulness, in the path of ministry. If you give a wider platform, so be it. But let our hearts live in the low places with others, with Jesus. In Jesus's name, amen.

THE QUESTIONS

- What are the low places in which you are serving right now? How do you sense the Holy Spirit moving in those settings?

36

IF (PART THREE)

LUKE 4:1–9

Jesus, full of the Holy Spirit, left the Jordan and was led by the Spirit into the wilderness, where for forty days he was tempted by the devil. He ate nothing during those days, and at the end of them he was hungry.

The devil said to him, "If you are the Son of God, tell this stone to become bread."

Jesus answered, "It is written: 'Man shall not live on bread alone.'"

The devil led him up to a high place and showed him in an instant all the kingdoms of the world. And he said to him, "I will give you all their authority and splendor; it has been given to me, and I can give it to anyone I want to. If you worship me, it will all be yours."

Jesus answered, "It is written: 'Worship the Lord your God and serve him only.'"

The devil led him to Jerusalem and had him stand on the highest point of the temple. "If you are the Son of God," he said, "throw yourself down from here."

CONSIDER THIS

If.

Here it is again. The enemy is relentless. The satan has all the time in the world to repeat the same attack again and again—but aiming that attack on the weakest point of your character, your faith, and your trust.

If.

"Jesus," the enemy says, "I'm just saying: If this Sonship thing is true, if its real, and you didn't mishear, misinterpret, and misunderstand what the Father said, then you should probably do a few tricks to prove yourself to him, to others, and to yourself. Perform, Jesus. Perform for your Father. Perform for all of us. Perform to convince yourself you are worth all the love you think has been invested in you."

Performance, it is well-known in the world of counseling, is a major barrier to becoming whole. We perform to get love. We perform to get acclaim. We perform to get those who should value us of their own accord, acting according to God's love for us, to give us affection and affirmation and adoration and attention.

We perform because we lack awareness of our belovedness. And loveless people, especially loveless Christians, can pull off performances for a good long while—until one day it all comes crumbling down in a personal breakdown, a relational crisis, or a highly visible public shaming (the worst nightmare for a performer).

Friends, we love him "because he first loved us" (1 John 4:19). Jesus tasted the sweetness of his belovedness, and his Son-shaped vocation, at his baptism. You and I can experience the same, and should be wary of leading if we aren't experiencing an ongoing, and I will even say "deeply emotional" connection with our Father who loves us.

THE PRAYER

Lord of the Wild, we admit that we have spent much of our lives performing to get love. There are times we wonder if we can quit the habit, seeking affirmation from you and others from what we do. Teach us what it means, in our emotions, to be loved and needed by you so we don't court the affections of the crowd or perform to get your love. We are loved as much as we will ever be in this moment, because of who we are—your precious children. In Jesus's name, amen.

THE QUESTIONS

- Can you name any areas of work or life in which you believe you have been performing in order to obtain love? What can you do to break out of the cycle?

37

YOU ARE THE SON OF GOD, HE SAID

LUKE 4:1–9

Jesus, full of the Holy Spirit, left the Jordan and was led by the Spirit into the wilderness, where for forty days he was tempted by the devil. He ate nothing during those days, and at the end of them he was hungry.

The devil said to him, "If you are the Son of God, tell this stone to become bread."

Jesus answered, "It is written: 'Man shall not live on bread alone.'"

The devil led him up to a high place and showed him in an instant all the kingdoms of the world. And he said to him, "I will give you all their authority and splendor; it has been given to me, and I can give it to anyone I want to. If you worship me, it will all be yours."

Jesus answered, "It is written: 'Worship the Lord your God and serve him only.'"

The devil led him to Jerusalem and had him stand on the highest point of the temple. "If *you are the Son of God,*" *he said,* "throw yourself down from here."

CONSIDER THIS

Within the third temptation of Jesus lies an issue of vocation, yours and mine, that our Lord had to face down so we could face it down behind him: *trust.*

Trust? Trust is acting on the belief that who God says you are, is who you actually are. Trust is believing that the Father's naming of you, and the purpose it carries, is enough.

Trust that has *nothing to prove*, no need to be validated.

Being the Son of God *and* the Son of Man couldn't have been easy. You are somewhere between flesh and blood and heavenly reality; seeing what is seen by all and seeing what is unseen by others. You are alive to God yet alive to self, present to divine communion and present to earthly desires. You are a place where heaven and earth meet, and you will be the firstborn from the dead—while knowing that death is final unless a will beyond you intervenes.

Before Jesus will step into the wild of his Isaiah 61 ministry, he will have to decide something: Does he trust his Father's plan, and does he really believe as the Son of God he will be caught if he falls?

For you and me, it is different, but no different, at the same time. We must trust God. We must. If we don't, we will live safely behind our home and church walls, talking about the easy themes of virtue and morality, while leaving all the risk-taking and Holy Spirit–following to those who are the real spiritual superstars. We will sigh over the news, nod our head at church, or perhaps lob a social media post into the fray (of our social media echo chamber, that group of people who are selected by algorithm to largely agree with what we say) of public opinion.

But we will not truly *live*.

We will certainly not live as a follower of Jesus.

Many years ago, I commissioned a student of mine to write a quote, in calligraphy, on the wall of my office. It was from early church Bishop Irenaeus of Lyon, and it said, "The glory of God is a human being, fully alive."

If we're going to follow Jesus, we're going to have to trust who he and the Father and the Spirit have said we are: beloved, chosen, royal priest, living sacrifice, child of God. Then, we're going to have to risk something, to actually trust, knowing it could cost us our lives.

We've got nothing to prove.

But we do have a life to live. Our name carries our purpose. The name "child of God" carries with it a purpose and a destiny to be lived, not hid or destroyed early because we have something to prove.

Let's do that. Today.

Let's live, fully alive in the presence of God.

THE PRAYER

Lord of the Wild, we have nothing to prove to anyone. We are your children, and we trust you. In Jesus's name, amen.

THE QUESTIONS

- How have you lived like you have something to prove in the world, like you need validation to assure you that you matter and are needed? How might the Father want to speak into this way you are living and seeking affirmation?

THROW YOURSELF
DOWN FROM HERE

LUKE 4:1–9

Jesus, full of the Holy Spirit, left the Jordan and was led by the Spirit into the wilderness, where for forty days he was tempted by the devil. He ate nothing during those days, and at the end of them he was hungry.

The devil said to him, "If you are the Son of God,
tell this stone to become bread."

Jesus answered, "It is written: 'Man shall not live on bread alone.'"

The devil led him up to a high place and showed him in an instant all the kingdoms of the world. And he said to him, "I will give you all their authority and splendor; it has been given to me, and I can give it to anyone I want to. If you worship me, it will all be yours."

Jesus answered, "It is written: 'Worship the Lord
your God and serve him only.'"

The devil led him to Jerusalem and had him stand on the highest point of the temple. "If you are the Son of God," he said, *"throw yourself down from here."*

CONSIDER THIS

Let's review. The temptation in the wild could also be called the testing in the wild, as Jesus is being tested as to his vocation in between his receiving it at his baptism and his actualizing of it in his Isaiah 61 ministry. He is full of the Holy Spirit and led by the Spirit into the wild. He is fasting, a spiritual practice common to those wanting to come close to God and to become more aware of God's presence as we become less focused on our bodily needs. In the wild, three temptations come his way from the one the Bible calls the satan, the accuser, the evil one—the devil.

The first test (I use this word interchangeably with temptation, as it depends on where we think the challenge is ultimately coming from) is a call for Jesus to misuse his power for personal gain.

The second test is a call for Jesus to skip over suffering and to take control of the world and its benefits.

The third test, a wild card, is a call for Jesus to manipulate God and to put on a show with his abilities.

So here we are, the third test in, with Jesus bearing a vocation to be the Son of God in all its fullness, the Suffering Servant of Isaiah 53, to bring "good news to the poor" (Isa. 61:1; Luke 4:18) and to "destroy the works of the evil one" (1 John 3:8), and the enemy is taking one last, ministry-sabotaging swing.

Jump and force the Father's hand. Instead of obedience, where you are yielded to the will of the Father, instead manipulate God to do *your* will.

It's the dark inverse of the Lord's Prayer: "My kingdom come. My will be done. In heaven as it is on earth." It is magic, the manipulation of spiritual position, to achieve by power what can only be achieved by selfless love.

Jesus had another version of "throw yourself down" in mind. He would throw himself down on his knees in the garden of

Gethsemane (to offer his will to the Father's, for the fullness of the Father's will to come to fruition).

Throw himself off the temple high place? Force God to catch him, to do his will outside of God's? To even risk his life and put his Isaiah 61 ministry and the deliverance of humankind on the line?

No. Jesus has no need to obey a satanic suggestion that puts a barrier between himself and his Father. Jesus will indeed throw himself down, on his knees, to offer the perfect and perfecting sacrifice for the world (Heb. 10:14).

His name means "the Lord saves." He's not going to risk that mission for a display—and he'll follow that same pattern many times over in his ministry to follow.

THE PRAYER

Lord of the Wild, there is something inside of us, still, that wants our wills to be done. We don't ultimately believe our will is better than yours, but honestly, your will and path feel hard and narrow and, at times, terrifying. Your kingdom come; your will be done—here in our lives as it is being done in heaven. In Jesus's name, amen.

THE QUESTIONS

- Have you ever been tempted to manipulate God to do your will? Has there been a time when God was moving too slowly and you acted, trusting he'd catch you even though you knew you weren't following his slow, patient time schedule?

IT IS WRITTEN (PART THREE)

LUKE 4:1–11

Jesus, full of the Holy Spirit, left the Jordan and was led by the Spirit into the wilderness, where for forty days he was tempted by the devil. He ate nothing during those days, and at the end of them he was hungry.

The devil said to him, "If you are the Son of God, tell this stone to become bread."

Jesus answered, "It is written: 'Man shall not live on bread alone.'"

The devil led him up to a high place and showed him in an instant all the kingdoms of the world. And he said to him, "I will give you all their authority and splendor; it has been given to me, and I can give it to anyone I want to. If you worship me, it will all be yours."

Jesus answered, "It is written: 'Worship the Lord your God and serve him only.'"

The devil led him to Jerusalem and had him stand on the highest point of the temple. "If you are the Son of God," he said, "throw yourself down from here. For *it is written*:

"'He will command his angels concerning you
to guard you carefully;
they will lift you up in their hands,
so that you will not strike your foot against a stone.'"

The third test, the third temptation, and the third response of Jesus. That response is the same one he has relied on each time the devil has approached, and if Jesus saw it as the most powerful way he could respond to temptation, then surely, we should learn that way ourselves.

I love to pray the Scriptures, and to get others to pray them with me. When we simply read Scripture, we can miss the personal power each passage has when declared back to God in prayer and worship.

When I answer the devil, and my own wayward heart, with "it is written," I am drawing on thousands of years of covenant history built around the lovingly delivered truth of God to humankind. When I pray the Scriptures in the face of testing or temptation, I am entering them—and they are entering me. When I pray the Scriptures, I am defining what is true not only for the devil before me, but for my own heart seeking to walk in the way of Jesus. When I pray the Scriptures, I am declaring that my own emotionally fragmented self will not offer enough good and true words to do battle for me.

When I pray the Scriptures, I am alive to God and God reveals himself to me.

There is no way around it; the Christian who does not hide the written Word of God in his or her heart has put down the sword of the Spirit in order to pick up a pocketknife for battle. There is no surviving the battle raging for our hearts without the sword of the Spirit, and the rest of the armor of God, protecting us along the way.

It bears reading Ephesians 6:10–18 (emphasis mine) out loud in order to get its truths settling in us as we respond to the enemy, "It is written," in the battles ahead:

> Finally, be strong in the Lord and in his mighty power. Put on the full armor of God, so that you can take your stand against the devil's schemes. For our struggle is not against flesh and blood, but against the rulers, against the authorities, against the powers of this dark world and against the spiritual forces of evil in the heavenly realms.
>
> Therefore put on the full armor of God, so that when the day of evil comes, you may be able to stand your ground, and after you have done everything, to stand. Stand firm then, with the belt of truth buckled around your waist, with the breastplate of righteousness in place, and with your feet fitted with the readiness that comes from the gospel of peace.
>
> In addition to all this, take up the shield of faith, with which you can extinguish all the flaming arrows of the evil one. Take the helmet of salvation and the *sword of the Spirit, which is the word of God.* And pray in the Spirit on all occasions with all kinds of prayers and requests.

You and I will make it if we always have the Word of the Lord hidden in our hearts with which we can respond with holy fire to the evil one.

THE PRAYER

Lord of the Wild, we are committed to committing the Word of God to heart. We know how important it has been to us to cling to your Word in times of trouble in the past; help us prepare for the future and the hiding of your Word in our hearts we will need in times to come. In Jesus's name, amen.

THE QUESTIONS

- Do you have a psalm to which you return again and again when facing down temptation or rising in faith to tests? Which one is it, and what words in the psalm most strengthen you during a challenge?

40

HE WILL COMMAND HIS ANGELS CONCERNING YOU

LUKE 4:1–11

Jesus, full of the Holy Spirit, left the Jordan and was led by the Spirit into the wilderness, where for forty days he was tempted by the devil. He ate nothing during those days, and at the end of them he was hungry.

The devil said to him, "If you are the Son of God, tell this stone to become bread."

Jesus answered, "It is written: 'Man shall not live on bread alone.'"

The devil led him up to a high place and showed him in an instant all the kingdoms of the world. And he said to him, "I will give you all their authority and splendor; it has been given to me, and I can give it to anyone I want to. If you worship me, it will all be yours."

Jesus answered, "It is written: 'Worship the Lord your God and serve him only.'"

The devil led him to Jerusalem and had him stand on the highest point of the temple. "If you are the Son of God," he said, "throw yourself down from here. For it is written:

"*'He will command his angels concerning you*
to guard you carefully;
they will lift you up in their hands,
so that you will not strike your foot against a stone.'"

I have a long history with angels. By that, I don't mean that I have angel posters and placards on my walls, or that I have experienced visitations of angels or visibly encountered spiritual beings.

What I mean is that I have a long history thinking about angels, considering angels, and seeking to understand how to even begin to think about spiritual beings. I believe that such a history, which predates me coming to faith in Jesus, was triggered by myriad spiritual experiences for which I had no explanation other than some mysterious powers at work.

I grew up with extended family members hanging strange, ethereal angel images on their paneled walls (one, if I recall correctly, was beside an old clock taken from a local bar). I even remember the first time I saw an image from Dante's *Inferno*, and thinking, *Angels and aliens; what if there is no difference?* A few bands from the '70s and '80s were clearly asking the same question.

In Colossians 2:18 we read: "Do not let anyone who delights in false humility and the worship of angels disqualify you. Such a person also goes into great detail about what they have seen; they are puffed up with idle notions by their unspiritual mind." Angels are not supposed to be a central focus for the believer; Jesus is. But we are to be aware they are present and active on our behalf.

But Jesus spoke of angels, from the Greek word which means "messengers," being about the Father's work in the world. Wouldn't it have been wonderful to see what Jesus saw as he ministered to the people and preached the good news of Luke 4 to the individual and to the masses? Wouldn't it have been startling to perceive the demonic at work in an almost visible way, or to perceive the angelic beings at work on behalf of the children ("See that you do not despise one of these little ones. For I tell you that their angels in heaven always see the face of my Father in heaven" [Matt. 18:10])?

Jesus was not walking alone through this world. Yes, the Father and the Spirit were with him. Yes, his disciples were close by. Yes, Jesus had crowds following him. In Matthew 4:11, another passage about Jesus in the wild, we read that when Jesus's testing was complete, the "angels came and attended him."

You and I are surrounded by "a great cloud of witnesses" cheering us on (Heb. 12:1) and by angels attending us along our journey (Heb. 1:14). Jesus was ministered to by angels, and so are we. With our singular focus on worshipping God as Father, Son, and Holy Spirit, and our prayers directed to God without distraction, we can know that the Lord is sending angels, messengers, to encourage us along our journey home.

THE PRAYER

Lord of the Wild, there is joy in knowing that we are not alone on this journey. We are filled with you, present in us and with us. You've given us companions and the community of saints for encouragement. And there are also ministering angels attending to us all along the way. We bless you for caring for us so. In Jesus's name, amen.

THE QUESTIONS

- While the Bible encourages us not to focus on angelic or spiritual beings, we are told they exist and are at work in the world. Can you think of a circumstance where you felt like you were cared for in a way that went far beyond what you could have hoped for? What happened?

41

JESUS ANSWERED
(PART THREE)

LUKE 4:1–12

Jesus, full of the Holy Spirit, left the Jordan and was led by the Spirit into the wilderness, where for forty days he was tempted by the devil. He ate nothing during those days, and at the end of them he was hungry.

The devil said to him, "If you are the Son of God, tell this stone to become bread."

Jesus answered, "It is written: 'Man shall not live on bread alone.'"

The devil led him up to a high place and showed him in an instant all the kingdoms of the world. And he said to him, "I will give you all their authority and splendor; it has been given to me, and I can give it to anyone I want to. If you worship me, it will all be yours."

Jesus answered, "It is written: 'Worship the Lord your God and serve him only.'"

The devil led him to Jerusalem and had him stand on the highest point of the temple. "If you are the Son of God," he said, "throw yourself down from here. For it is written:

"'He will command his angels concerning you
to guard you carefully;
they will lift you up in their hands,
so that you will not strike your foot against a stone.'"

Jesus answered, "It is said: 'Do not put the Lord your God to the test.'"

The word for Jesus "answered," in Greek, literally means that Jesus "responded to the present, now, current situation." In other words, Jesus was in a moment of challenge, and he had an immediate response.

Delayed responses to God mean *disobedience*, according to the Scriptures. Delayed responses to the devil mean *acquiescence*.

In the former case, a delay in obedience means that we are trusting ourselves more than God and believe that delaying a response of obedience will enable us to escape suffering in our discipleship (the second temptation all over again).

In the latter case, a delay when facing temptation means that we are trusting ourselves more than is wise, allowing the enemy to get a foothold in our hearts. We are called to *turn* from evil (Ps. 34:14, 37:27; 1 Peter 3:11), to *run* from evil, so we don't give it a second chance to grab ahold of our desires.

Second Peter 2:20 suggest that if we delay in refusing what the enemy is offering, we can do virtually irreparable damage to our souls: "If they have escaped the corruption of the world by knowing our Lord and Savior Jesus Christ and are again entangled in it and are overcome, they are worse off at the end than they were at the beginning."

I remember a moment right after coming to faith at university that an old temptation came my way. In the moment it was presented, I felt that old, familiar draw to take the bait and welcome the pull for a little while.

But the Spirit helped me with a single word: *run.*

It was loud in my spirit; it came as a command rather than as a suggestion or quiet intuition.

I didn't excuse myself; I didn't try to make small talk to remove the awkwardness of the situation. I just turned and left. I am so glad I did. A vortex of hell was waiting for me, and Jesus spoke to me later: "We've come too far to go back."

We can recount circumstances in our lives when we failed to answer, quickly, in the moment, and have either faced repercussions we wish we had avoided or missed opportunities to convey God's love in a powerful way.

When God speaks, answer quickly. When the devil speaks, answer quickly. A delay can cost us more than time.

THE PRAYER

Lord of the Wild, we fear in moments of obedience or temptation that we will be out of control. Minister to our spirits so our trust leads our indecision and lead us to faithfulness. In Jesus's name, amen.

THE QUESTIONS

- Can you recount a circumstance where you delayed obedience, and experienced a missed opportunity? What happened and how did you return to obedience?

IT IS SAID

LUKE 4:1–12

Jesus, full of the Holy Spirit, left the Jordan and was led by the Spirit into the wilderness, where for forty days he was tempted by the devil. He ate nothing during those days, and at the end of them he was hungry.

The devil said to him, "If you are the Son of God, tell this stone to become bread."

Jesus answered, "It is written: 'Man shall not live on bread alone.'"

The devil led him up to a high place and showed him in an instant all the kingdoms of the world. And he said to him, "I will give you all their authority and splendor; it has been given to me, and I can give it to anyone I want to. If you worship me, it will all be yours."

Jesus answered, "It is written: 'Worship the Lord your God and serve him only.'"

The devil led him to Jerusalem and had him stand on the highest point of the temple. "If you are the Son of God," he said, "throw yourself down from here. For it is written:

"'He will command his angels concerning you to guard you carefully; they will lift you up in their hands, so that you will not strike your foot against a stone.'"

Jesus answered, "*It is said*: 'Do not put the Lord your God to the test.'"

In human relationships, it is very important who said what in a conversation. We infer motives when someone says something, and we are surprised or not surprised when someone says something, knowing who they are and what they have been through.

Jesus, in this moment, was calling on the entirety of the covenant community of Israel when he said the words, "It is said."

"It is said by whom?" the reader, and even the devil, may ask. To answer this question, we must go back to the passage in Deuteronomy to which Jesus is referring.

Deuteronomy 6:14–19 (emphasis mine) says:

> Do not follow other gods, the gods of the peoples around you; for the LORD your God, who is among you, is a jealous God and his anger will burn against you, and he will destroy you from the face of the land. *Do not put the LORD your God to the test as you did at Massah.* Be sure to keep the commands of the LORD your God and the stipulations and decrees he has given you. Do what is right and good in the LORD's sight, so that it may go well with you and you may go in and take over the good land the LORD promised on oath to your ancestors, thrusting out all your enemies before you, as the LORD said.

Who put the Lord their God to the test at Massah? The Israelites, God's people, that's who. At Massah (*testing*) and Meribah (*quarreling*) the chosen of God demanded water, testing God and Moses, quarreling all along the way.

Resisting God leads to eventual devastation and lessons learned.

In Exodus 17:7 we read: "And he [Moses] called the place Massah and Meribah because the Israelites quarreled and because they tested the LORD saying, 'Is the LORD among us or not?'"

Moses, on behalf of God's entire covenant family across time, and repeated by their children's children across history, is the one who is behind the "It is said" in Jesus's response to the enemy.

And here we find a reason to speak Scripture, pray Scripture, and respond with Scripture. We are leveraging that mass of spiritual equity of the faithful who have gone before us in their response to God, as we respond to our foe.

— But did they really? They kept on doing it until...

The Israelites learned a lesson at Massah and Meribah, and they repeated the story of that lesson throughout time in the form of a command from the Lord.

Jesus called that entire corporate movement of covenant journey with God to mind with the three simple words, "It is said." "Our words" in resisting the enemy may need to be replaced with "Our Words" of the entire covenant community. There is a difference.

THE PRAYER

Lord of the Wild, we thank you for all the lessons of your covenant people that have preceded our own situations, and for the wisdom from which we can draw. May we not test you as the people of Israel tested you. Let our daily response be one of immediate, and blessed, obedience. In Jesus's name, amen.

- Have you ever spoken back to the enemy, in the face of a moment of temptation, using the Scriptures and the weight of your covenant family's response to God? What was that moment like, and what Scripture did you use?

DO NOT PUT THE LORD YOUR GOD TO THE TEST

LUKE 4:1–12

Jesus, full of the Holy Spirit, left the Jordan and was led by the Spirit into the wilderness, where for forty days he was tempted by the devil. He ate nothing during those days, and at the end of them he was hungry.

The devil said to him, "If you are the Son of God, tell this stone to become bread."

Jesus answered, "It is written: 'Man shall not live on bread alone.'"

The devil led him up to a high place and showed him in an instant all the kingdoms of the world. And he said to him, "I will give you all their authority and splendor; it has been given to me, and I can give it to anyone I want to. If you worship me, it will all be yours."

Jesus answered, "It is written: 'Worship the Lord your God and serve him only.'"

The devil led him to Jerusalem and had him stand on the highest point of the temple. "If you are the Son of God," he said, "throw yourself down from here. For it is written:

"'He will command his angels concerning you
to guard you carefully;
they will lift you up in their hands,
so that you will not strike your foot against a stone.'"

Jesus answered, "It is said: '*Do not put the Lord your God to the test*.'"

I had a recent experience where, in a close relationship, I was put to the test. I was acting in integrity, seeking to move in humility, and yet I was continually being opposed by someone not in a good place.

I finally said, "Stop putting me to the test." I was at the end of my patience. I felt the blessing of God to put an end to the circular conversation and to make a stand that would move us forward.

Jesus, recalling Israel's testing of God at Massah and Meribah, will not conspire with the devil to put the Lord God to the test. In other words, Jesus will not test God's patience, God's promise, or God's love.

He will do the will of the Father without question. He will not ask the Father to perform a miracle that is based on Jesus's will rather than the will of the Father. He will not manipulate God. He will not grumble or quarrel or complain about God's timing, actions, or plans.

Jesus will not put the Lord his God to the test.

I am glad that God is full of grace toward me and toward you. He lives up to his words on love, spoken through Paul: "Love is patient, love is kind. It does not envy, it does not boast, it is not proud. It does not dishonor others, it is not self-seeking, it is not easily angered, it keeps no record of wrongs. Love does not delight in evil but rejoices with the truth. It always protects, always trusts, always hopes, always perseveres" (1 Cor. 13:4–7).

Even in the face of such faithfulness and love, I still put God to the test. I am stiff-necked in my worst moments, untrusting, and a worrier. Still, the Father hangs in there with me.

Jesus is doing what Israel could not do, in order to work in you and me what only Jesus could do—obey the Father in fullness and completeness.

Jesus, representing the nation of Israel as the Second Adam, and the bearer of the new covenant, will obey.

The breach will be fixed, the gap will be closed.

You and I can live in such a way that we do not test God—rather, we bless him.

THE PRAYER

Lord of the Wild, we know what it is to test God. We sense impatience and fear, even now, rising in our hearts due to circumstances out of our control. Teach us to trust you through the storms, to remain a believer in the rough times as well as the smooth. In Jesus's name, amen.

THE QUESTION

- In what ways have you recently experienced God being gracious with you—not withholding his love even though you were pushing the boundaries of his patience and promise?

WHEN THE DEVIL HAD FINISHED ALL THIS TEMPTING

LUKE 4:1–12

Jesus, full of the Holy Spirit, left the Jordan and was led by the Spirit into the wilderness, where for forty days he was tempted by the devil. He ate nothing during those days, and at the end of them he was hungry.

The devil said to him, "If you are the Son of God, tell this stone to become bread."

Jesus answered, "It is written: 'Man shall not live on bread alone.'"

The devil led him up to a high place and showed him in an instant all the kingdoms of the world. And he said to him, "I will give you all their authority and splendor; it has been given to me, and I can give it to anyone I want to. If you worship me, it will all be yours."

Jesus answered, "It is written: 'Worship the Lord your God and serve him only.'"

The devil led him to Jerusalem and had him stand on the highest point of the temple. "If you are the Son of God," he said, "throw yourself down from here. For it is written:

"'He will command his angels concerning you to guard you carefully; they will lift you up in their hands, so that you will not strike your foot against a stone.'"

Jesus answered, "It is said: 'Do not put the Lord your God to the test.'"

When the devil had finished all this tempting,
he left him until an opportune time.

CONSIDER THIS

Forty days, three temptations, and three vocationally charged answers later, the devil walks away from the battle. In other words, the devil calls it quits on the *game*—but is not calling it quits on the *season.*

There are seasons of relief in our battle with the adversary of our souls—and for those, we can be grateful. When we fall to temptation, the season that follows is often filled with strife, anxiety, conflict, and even full breaks in life as we know it.

But when we face temptation and overcome it, and the Lord and we have seen our faith, "of greater worth than gold," tested and proved genuine (1 Peter 1:7), there may be a time of reprieve when we can regroup and get ready for the next phase of ministry.

Jesus has been baptized, and his vocation and personhood have been affirmed. He goes into the wild to face temptation, to be tested, as to his deep ownership of that vocation. And he will come out of the wild ready to preach good news to the poor, freedom to the captives, and "to proclaim the year of the Lord's favor" (Luke 4:18–19).

The devil threw his best at Jesus, aiming to get him questioning if he was indeed the Son of God; to get him reconsidering the use of his power to serve himself, or the status of his belovedness to skip suffering and inherit glittering kingdoms; and to test his relationship with God (his God-security).

At every turn, Jesus has resisted the enemy by using the Word of God, the story of the saints, and by reinforcing the Father's love for him by recalling the truths of his promises.

So there is an end to seasons of temptation, seasons of testing, and we can trust there is another side when we feel trapped on one side of a storm.

Today, is there a season of temptation or testing you feel you are in, that is pushing you to the edge of your strength and challenging your capacity to bear it?

The Lord says there will be an end to this season. Be strong and courageous, recall and reclaim his Word, and there will be a time when, we trust and hope, it is over and there is some reprieve. Just remain faithful through it, no matter how long it takes.

THE PRAYER

Lord of the Wild, there is distress in seasons when we are pushed to our very limits. We may be in one right now, and we choose to stay the course without lingering in doubt or challenging your faithfulness. Take us to our limits, that we may become limitless in our trust in you for the years to come. In Jesus's name, amen.

THE QUESTIONS

- Have you ever been stretched to your limit in your trust of God? How did you emerge on the other side?

HE LEFT HIM UNTIL AN OPPORTUNE TIME

LUKE 4:1–12

Jesus, full of the Holy Spirit, left the Jordan and was led by the Spirit into the wilderness, where for forty days he was tempted by the devil. He ate nothing during those days, and at the end of them he was hungry.

The devil said to him, "If you are the Son of God,
tell this stone to become bread."

Jesus answered, "It is written: 'Man shall not live on bread alone.'"

The devil led him up to a high place and showed him in an instant all the kingdoms of the world. And he said to him, "I will give you all their authority and splendor; it has been given to me, and I can give it to anyone I want to. If you worship me, it will all be yours."

Jesus answered, "It is written: 'Worship the Lord
your God and serve him only.'"

The devil led him to Jerusalem and had him stand on the highest point of the temple. "If you are the Son of God," he said, "throw yourself down from here. For it is written:

"'He will command his angels concerning you
to guard you carefully;
they will lift you up in their hands,
so that you will not strike your foot against a stone.'"

Jesus answered, "It is said: 'Do not put the Lord your God to the test.'"

When the devil had finished all this tempting,
he left him until an opportune time.

What is an opportune time for the devil to tempt us, push us, demean us, question our name or our purpose or our calling before God?

It is certainly not when we are strong. The enemy will look for a time when we are the most under pressure, the most vulnerable, the most tired, to attack. And that attack will be subtle, often marked less by direct frontal assaults and more by inner questions like: "If you are loved by God, then why is this happening to you?"

Has the enemy of your soul walked away from you recently, knowing he has been beaten? Has evil recently taken its leave of you, knowing you will not succumb and that you are firmly established in your trust of God?

If so, hallelujah! Well done! Way to go! The Lord reigns! "He who began a good work in you" will be faithful to complete it to the day of Christ Jesus (Phil. 1:6)!

But know this: the adversary will come at you again, and this side of heaven, you will not be off the battlefield until the war for your heart, and the hearts of humankind, is won. There is a rest ahead for you and for the people of God: "There remains, then, a Sabbath-rest for the people of God; for anyone who enters God's rest also rests from their works, just as God did from his. Let us, therefore, make every effort to enter that rest" (Heb. 4:9–11).

Immediately following this promise of rest, we are called to hold onto our weapon; the battle is still raging, so we don't want to get lost in the dream of the future while the swords of the evil one are headed our way: "For the word of God is alive and active. Sharper than any double-edged sword, it penetrates even to dividing soul and spirit, joints and marrow; it judges the thoughts and attitudes of the heart" (Heb. 4:12).

Your vocation, your calling, your name and mission as a child of God is under an onslaught of the enemy's creation; while you live and breathe, though there may be reprieves along the way, the enemy of your soul is waiting for "an opportune time."

When you are tired, run down, feeling anxious, or wondering if you can resist the temptations that may lie ahead, that is the time to worship, to reinforce weekly community relationships (banded discipleship is the way forward—see discipleshipbands.com), to stay alert, to keep your spiritual wits about you, and to frequently and multiple times daily engage spiritual practices that keep you in the baptismal love that Jesus experienced.

Rehearse your belovedness, know your calling as a child of God; the devil is waiting around a corner for the next vulnerable moment to attack.

THE PRAYER

Lord of the Wild, once again we take confidence that you are with us on this battlefield of the heart on which we find ourselves. There is no place we would rather be than at your side as the difficulties come our way. Teach us to use the sword of the Spirit, the Word of God, that is sharper than any double-edged sword, as we resist the promises of sin. In Jesus's name, amen.

- Can you name the times when your guard is most down related to the enemy seeking to trip you up? What are the circumstances in which you feel the most vulnerable to succumbing to the enemy's schemes to derail you, and what can you do to reinforce your line at those times?

46

JESUS RETURNED TO GALILEE IN THE POWER OF THE SPIRIT

LUKE 4:1–12

Jesus, full of the Holy Spirit, left the Jordan and was led by the Spirit into the wilderness, where for forty days he was tempted by the devil. He ate nothing during those days, and at the end of them he was hungry.

The devil said to him, "If you are the Son of God, tell this stone to become bread."

Jesus answered, "It is written: 'Man shall not live on bread alone.'"

The devil led him up to a high place and showed him in an instant all the kingdoms of the world. And he said to him, "I will give you all their authority and splendor; it has been given to me, and I can give it to anyone I want to. If you worship me, it will all be yours."

Jesus answered, "It is written: 'Worship the Lord your God and serve him only.'"

The devil led him to Jerusalem and had him stand on the highest point of the temple. "If you are the Son of God," he said, "throw yourself down from here. For it is written:

"'He will command his angels concerning you
to guard you carefully;
they will lift you up in their hands,
so that you will not strike your foot against a stone.'"

Jesus answered, "It is said: 'Do not put the Lord your God to the test.'"

When the devil had finished all this tempting,
he left him until an opportune time.

Jesus returned to Galilee in the power of the Spirit, and
news about him spread through the whole countryside.

CONSIDER THIS

Jesus faces down the temptations that Israel could not, the tests of faith that Israel could not, and emerges from his long season of fasting and faith-reinforcing "in the power of the Spirit."

There is a benefit to being tested, and God knows what we do not. On the other side of a test passed is a pure, glowing, world-bending *spiritual resilience*.

Let's talk about spiritual resilience in such times as we live. Resilience speaks of the ability to face an impact and to recover quickly from its force. There is a spiritual elasticity inherent to resilience; we take hits but have the ability for them to bounce off us without damage. In fact, the most resilient and elastic of people can use the momentum with which they've been hit and turn its energy back on the enemy.

Jesus comes out of his season of vocational testing knowing whose he is, who he is, and what he is for. I think coming out of the wild "in the power of the Spirit" (v. 14), for you and me, means we have faced down that inner voice of temptation in this round (v. 13) and we have had our faith proved genuine, at the very least, to ourselves (1 Peter 1:6–9).

We will all have many opportunities in the wild, the unpredictable, the surprising circumstances of life, to face down the challenger. Our suffering, our vulnerable places, can be places we enter with our unspoken-name-written-on-a-white-stone (see Rev. 2:17) in our hearts and we do battle with word and Word.

My prayers are with us in the unresolved, and in the battle for our true names in Christ to be lived this side of eternity.

James 4:7–10 can help us for today:

> Submit yourselves, then, to God. Resist the devil, and he will flee from you. Come near to God and he will come near to you. Wash your hands, you sinners, and purify your hearts, you double-minded. Grieve, mourn and wail. Change your laughter to mourning and your joy to gloom. Humble yourselves before the Lord, and he will lift you up.

Here's to knowing whose we are, who we are, and why we are—as we follow Jesus into the wild.

THE PRAYER

Lord of the Wild, we have come to the place where living "in the power of the Spirit" is both our priority and our desire. Fill us with your Spirit for the challenges ahead, even today, and give us a deepening sense of your abiding presence as we address the enemy's taunts. In Jesus's name, amen.

THE QUESTIONS

- What is your favorite phrase or verse in James 4:7–10? Why?

47

AND NEWS ABOUT HIM SPREAD THROUGH THE WHOLE COUNTRYSIDE

LUKE 4:1–12

Jesus, full of the Holy Spirit, left the Jordan and was led by the Spirit into the wilderness, where for forty days he was tempted by the devil. He ate nothing during those days, and at the end of them he was hungry.

The devil said to him, "If you are the Son of God, tell this stone to become bread."

Jesus answered, "It is written: 'Man shall not live on bread alone.'"

The devil led him up to a high place and showed him in an instant all the kingdoms of the world. And he said to him, "I will give you all their authority and splendor; it has been given to me, and I can give it to anyone I want to. If you worship me, it will all be yours."

Jesus answered, "It is written: 'Worship the Lord your God and serve him only.'"

The devil led him to Jerusalem and had him stand on the highest point of the temple. "If you are the Son of God," he said, "throw yourself down from here. For it is written:

"'He will command his angels concerning you to guard you carefully; they will lift you up in their hands, so that you will not strike your foot against a stone.'"

Jesus answered, "It is said: 'Do not put the Lord your God to the test.'"

> When the devil had finished all this tempting,
> he left him until an opportune time.
>
> Jesus returned to Galilee in the power of the Spirit, *and news about him spread through the whole countryside.*

CONSIDER THIS

In Genesis 32:28 we read about Jesus's forefather, Jacob, whose name became Israel: "Then the man said, 'Your name will no longer be Jacob, but Israel, because you have struggled with God and with humans and have overcome.'"

Jesus, on behalf of Israel, overcomes the enemy and the temptations of evil in the wild. He is pressed on every side, and the adversary has the singular agenda of snuffing Jesus out—by crushing his name, disorienting him from love, and ultimately getting him to take his own life before he offers it for the world.

But Jesus's inner life proves to be too mature, too beloved, too self-aware, too spiritually resilient, too formed by the deep and steady spiritual practices of his people, to devour.

- An encounter with the love of the Father made Jesus impenetrable.

- Sabbath rest and renewal made Jesus formidable.

- Daily prayer habits made Jesus unswayable.

- Daily Scripture reading habits made Jesus unconfuseable.

- Daily songs of worship, rolling in his spirit from the Psalms, the prayer book of his people Israel, made Jesus undistractable.

On the other side of his victory over the enemy's affront, doing in forty days what Israel could not in forty years, Jesus comes out not only unscathed but also "in the power of the Spirit" (Luke 4:14). He is full of dynamic, spiritual energy—energy that will be laser-focused on living out the message of Luke 4:18–19 (from Isaiah 61:1–2 and 58:6): "The Spirit of the Lord is on me, because he has anointed me to proclaim good news to the poor. He has sent me to proclaim freedom for the prisoners and recovery of sight for the blind, to set the oppressed free, to proclaim the year of the Lord's favor."

It was Jesus's inner life, built up by an ongoing encounter with the Father reinforced by spiritual habits that were nonnegotiables in Jesus's life, that enabled him to move into the ultimate of human ministries to undo the works of the evil one (1 John 3:8).

When the enemy faced Jesus in the wild, there was no spiritual sinkhole, no hollow heart, within Jesus to leverage.

When we come out of the wild having faced the enemy and resisted, having faced a test and been found faithful, good news will spread. People will meet a person who has strengthened their own weak knees and quivering heart through a growing, cultivated intimacy with God—and the hearts, homes, churches, and cities around us will be changed.

THE PRAYER

Lord of the Wild, we want to become good news in Jesus's name. Help us establish ourselves in inner habits that prepare us for temptation and equip us to face our challenges. We want nothing less than all of you moving in and through all of us in the world you love. In Jesus's name, amen.

THE QUESTION

- Do you have spiritual habits that reinforce your daily sense of belovedness, that keep you in the Word and in prayer, and that make you a force to be reckoned with?

THE SOWER'S CREED

Today,

I sow for a great awakening.

Today,

I stake everything on the promise of the Word of God.

I depend entirely on the power of the Holy Spirit.

I have the same mind in me that was in Christ Jesus.

Because Jesus is good news and Jesus
is in me, I am good news.

Today,

I will sow the extravagance of the gospel
everywhere I go and into everyone I meet.

Today,

I will love others as Jesus has loved me.

Today,

I will remember that the tiniest seeds become the tallest trees;

that the seeds of today become the shade of tomorrow;

that the faith of right now becomes the future of

the everlasting kingdom.

Today,

I sow for a great awakening.